OUTLOOK
LEADERSHIP 2010

MARS
chocolate
north america

This copy of *Risk, Originality & Virtuosity: The Keys to a Perfect 10* by Peter Vidmar is presented by MARS Chocolate North America

THOUGHTS OR COMMENTS FOR US? TEXT OR EMAIL THEM TO FEEDBACK@CSPNET.COM

AUGUST 22 – 24, 2010 | GRAND AMERICA HOTEL | SALT LAKE CITY, UTAH

RISK, ORIGINALITY & VIRTUOSITY

(R.O.V.)

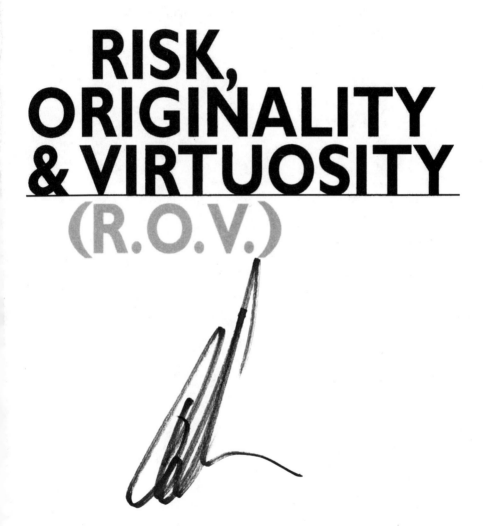

Also by Peter Vidmar, in collaboration with others,

Awaken the Olympian Within: Stories from America's Greatest Olympic Motivators

RISK, ORIGINALITY & VIRTUOSITY
(R.O.V.)

The Keys to a Perfect 10

Peter Vidmar

i𝑝M
INTERNATIONAL PUBLISHERS MARKETING

Distributed by i𝒑M

INTERNATIONAL PUBLISHERS MARKETING

International Publishers Marketing
22841 Quicksilver Drive
Sterling, Virgina 20166
800-758-3756
www.internationalpubmarket.com

ISBN 0-9710078-5-3 (alk.paper)

Library of Congress Cataloging-in-Publication Data

Vidmar, Peter.
    Risk, originality & virtuosity (R.O.V.): the keys to a perfect 10
/ Peter Vidmar.—1st ed.
        p. cm.
    Includes index.
    ISBN 0-9710078-5-3
        1. Vidmar, Peter. 2. Gymnasts—United States—Biography.
3. Success. 4. Conduct of life. I. Title: Risk, originality, and
virtuosity (R.O.V.). II Title.
    GV460.2.V53 A3 2002
    796.44'092—dc21
    [B]   2002073031

Printed in Canada

First Edition

10 9 8 7 6 5 4

All the world's a stage.

WILLIAM SHAKESPEARE, *AS YOU LIKE IT*

Contents

Acknowledgments

This project actually began in the previous century, so I'm thrilled to see it completed before the next one. This would have been impossible without the work of Lee Benson. Lee came to see me speak years ago and began to put into writing many of the stories contained in this book. Lee, a walking library of Olympic history and trivia, gave this work more depth than I could possibly have given on my own.

My thanks to Olympic team coach Abe Grossfield for his incredible recall of even the most obscure gymnastics trivia.

Mark French and Matt Jones at Leading Authorities helped me to see this to completion. There is nothing like a deadline to get things done.

I owe a big Thank You to Holli Catchpole, Marsha Horshok, Abbe Steiger, and Erin Falk of SpeakersOffice. They are the best at what they do. Their management of my speaking business gave me the time to finish *R.O.V.*

My life in sport has been an incredible journey, enriched by the close bond of my Olympic teammates, Tim Daggett, Mitch Gaylord, Jim Hartung, Bart Conner, and Scott Johnson. Standing on the Olympic podium was an amazing experience, and standing with my teammates was indescribable.

The really important lessons I learned in sport, I learned from Makoto Sakamoto. You will see this as you read the book. I cannot repay him for all he's done for me.

Finally, I thank my wife of nearly twenty years, Donna, for her love and understanding throughout these many years.

Our children—Timothy, Christopher, Stephen, Kathryn, and Emily—are worth more than all the gold in the world. I thank God every day for the most beautiful blessings He continues to give.

Introduction: Just Perfect

It was at the 1976 Olympic Games in Montreal that Nadia Comaneci, a 14-year-old Romanian schoolgirl, did something Olympic gymnasts to that point had only dreamed about: She stumped the judges.

For all of you competitors out there, no matter what your interest, you know what I'm talking about. Beyond the thrill of victory, way beyond the agony of defeat, there's the Moment You Baffle the System. When the stars and the planets line up just right. When you've got them where you want them and they know it. It's the feeling Paul Newman had in *Hombre* when he said to Richard Boone, *"I've got a question for you! How are you going to get back down that hill?"* It's what Joe Namath felt at the end of Super Bowl III, when he realized his guarantee really was a guarantee *and there wasn't anything they could do about it!* It happened in the 2001 Tour de France, when Lance Armstrong, after faking fatigue, took one look behind and stared down his nemesis Jan Ullrich, then launched up the infamous Alpe d'Huez, tearing off the legs of every other rider.

Well, that's how Nadia, all 86 pounds of her, felt. She had the Montreal judges in a quandary.

They couldn't find anything wrong with what she'd just done.

They were stunned all right. This had never before happened in the Olympics. There was always something to mark down a routine. A slip, a fall, a toe not pointed, a quick glance in the direction of the television cameras, a shaky dismount, a conservative dismount, an unplanned dismount. *Something.* If nothing else, there was always the need to cancel out the low score the judge from the Soviet Union was going to give. But this time there was nothing. This time the girl in pigtails wearing just the hint of a smile gave them no outs. She bewildered the panel. There she was in front of them, standing straight as a statue after an uneven bars routine the *Montreal Daily News & Citizen* would describe in its following morning's editions as "*flawless,*" and there they were, squirming in their official judge uniforms, fidgeting with their pencils, wrongfooted as it were, wading into the first stages of scoring shock.

But the judges of Montreal, to their credit, soon recovered. And even if they didn't want to, even if this meant they would go where no Olympic gymnastics judge had ever gone before—even if this meant they risked getting reputations as *easy grader*—they did what they knew they had to do. They gave the contestant from Romania the first flawless grade in the history of the Games. Full credit. Top marks. You couldn't score higher if you tried again a million times. You couldn't score higher if you gave every judge a Rolls Royce beforehand. You couldn't score higher in your dreams.

Just like that, perfection had a synonym.

"10.0."

"Ten point oh."

You could argue that this was the biggest moment in gymnastics history; bigger than Olga Korbut in the '72 Olympic Games; bigger than the Tsukahara vault; bigger than the debut of the iron cross; bigger than the invention of foam rubber.

"*Nadia Awed Ya*" trumpeted the headline in that week's *Sports Illustrated.*

Gymnastics suddenly had more converts than rock and roll. The world was enamored. *Where would you grade that on a scale of 1 to 10?* became an instant cliche. Hollywood made a movie about the world's most beautiful woman and titled it "10." Bo

Derek might not have known it, but she owed her career to a very flexible 4' 11" teenager from Onesti.

Nearly a half billion people who watched the Olympics that night on television knew they'd seen something unprecedented. Proof of that was verified when the Olympic officials, much to their chagrin, had to send for a technician to update the huge scorebord hanging from the roof of the Montreal Forum. The computerized scoreboard, like the Forum, was new for the 1976 Olympic Games and, as with everything else in those Games, the best that money could buy. That big scoreboard could display point totals down to the hundredths. It could list every name of every country entered in the Olympics. It had instant replay and stereo sound and revolving screens. It was state of the art. You could watch *Jeopardy* on it.

But there was one thing it couldn't do.

It couldn't display a "10."

Just like that, Nadia had rendered it obsolete. It could get to 9.99 and that was it. Officially, Nadia's score was recorded on the judge's clipboards just seconds following her picture perfect dismount. On paper she was a 10. But as far as the Forum scoreboard was concerned, it was a 1.0. She wasn't a 10 until the next morning, after they'd re-programmed the computer.

It was a good thing they changed the board, too, because that wasn't the end of it. Six more times in those Olympics Nadia Comaneci was "perfect." And yet another two 10's were added by Nelli Kim of the Soviet Union.

Once Nadia had shown the way, once she'd exposed a 10 as reachable, others, like Kim, were quick to step through the door of perfection. A door that was previously believed to be locked tight. Every Olympics since 1976 has seen its share of 10's. Where there were none for the first eighty years of the Olympic movement, by either the women or the men, suddenly they had become, if not exactly common, at least not unexpected.

Breaking Barriers

Sport has always served as a great allegory for human aspirations. There's something about scoreboards and stopwatches and yardsticks, and about the concrete, identifiable objectives they measure, that make it possible to better quantify the human experience; to distinguish what works from what doesn't.

Nadia took gymnasts through the "10" barrier much like Roger Bannister led milers through the four-minute mile barrier a couple of decades earlier. For years, milers had approached a 3:59-minute mile like medieval Spanish sailors once approached the ocean's horizon—always bracing for the moment when they'd fall off the edge and self-destruct. It just didn't seem doable, running a mile under four minutes, not for human beings, anyway, and year after year, track meet after track meet, that thinking kept getting reinforced. Milers would get only so close, and then they'd back off, as if they were afraid of falling off the edge.

Then along came the Englishman, Bannister, who, on May 6, 1954, put matter over mind and ran his historic 3:59.4.

Just like that, the stampede was on. Now you couldn't go to a track meet without somebody new limbo-ing under the four-minute bar. Within a year nearly a dozen more men had done it. The world mile record that had stayed stuck at 4:01 for more than ten years suddenly dropped like gravity. In a little more than three years it was lowered all the way to 3:54.5. In the decades since, the four-minute barrier has been broken literally thousands of times. My good friend, four-time Olympian Henry Marsh, the American record-holder in the 3,000-meter steeplechase, ran under four minutes at age thirty-five—and he wasn't even a miler!

Whatever the limit was for a human being running a mile, it *was not* four minutes. For showing the way, the British made Bannister a Sir.

The Right Step

Another man the British knighted for going where no one had gone before was the New Zealand mountain climber Sir Edmund Hillary, who, along with Tenzing Norgay of Nepal, became the first to climb the highest mountain on earth, Mount Everest, in 1953.

Until Hillary came along, the summit of Everest was considered insurmountable, and not just because, at 29,028 feet, it was at the same altitude most people associate with the announcement, *"We have reached our cruising height; you are now free to walk around the cabin and lower your seatbacks and tray tables."*

For climbers, a lack of oxygen wasn't Everest's biggest problem. That paled to a nasty stretch of ice and rock just below the summit that served as a kind of Everest Roadblock. The ice and rock sits at the top of a thin, forbidding mountain spine that, on a clear day, affords (so they say) fantastic views of Nepal and China. One is five miles to the left, the other five miles to the right. Straight down.

This spiny stretch of ice and rock frightened, and stumped, mountaineers for decades. They didn't know what to do with this "rock step," as Hillary called it in his book *Adventure's End.* Accomplished climbers would get this far and then, stumped, they'd stop, their goal just around the corner, but still out of reach.

Then along came Hillary. As he recounts in his book:

> "We were fast approaching the most formidable obstacle on the ridge—a great rock step. This step had always been visible in aerial photographs, and . . . we had always thought of it as the obstacle on the ridge which could well spell defeat. I looked anxiously up at the rocks. Planted squarely across the ridge in a vertical bluff, they looked extremely difficult, and I knew that our strength and ability to climb steep rock at this altitude would be severely limited . . . Search as I

could, I was unable to see an easy route up to the step or, in fact, any route at all. Finally, in desperation I examined the right-hand end of the bluff. Attached to this and overhanging the precipitous East face was a large cornice. This cornice . . . had started to lose its grip on the rock and a long narrow vertical crack had been formed between the rock and the ice. The crack was large enough to take the human frame, and though it offered little security, it was at least a route. I quickly made up my mind—it was worth a try."

And so Hillary went where no man had gone before. He gave something new a try, and once he'd used that "crack" to maneuver himself beyond the great rock step, the top of the world stretched out in front of him as if with open arms.

That portion of the final assault up Everest has been known as the *Hillary Step* ever since. It serves as a kind of litmus test to gain entrance to the earth's throne. One last awkward, challenging climb to make sure you've paid for the view. It's not easy. Getting to the top of the world—in anything—rarely is. But it *is* possible. That was Sir Edmund Hillary's gift to the world. He showed it could be done. In the half-century since he maneuvered his way through that rock step, more than six hundred people have conquered Mount Everest.

Of course, just knowing that something is reachable in no way guarantees its accomplishment. For proof of that, ask the more than five thousand climbers who have tried and come up short on Everest even after Hillary established his Step; or witness the recent tragedies of those who came ill-prepared. For that matter, ask those who haven't run the mile under four minutes—still a sizeable club, to be sure.

What It Takes

The positive experiences of others not only shows us what's possible, but by looking at their performances we can also understand what's necessary to get where they went. Whether we want to pay the price they paid is our own decision. But at the very least we have evidence of what has been done, and more importantly, what *can* be done.

For gymnasts, a dissection of Nadia Comaneci's routines in the days after Montreal revealed just what it was she'd done to score those seven perfect 10's.

There was no mystery to it. Under the scoring system of the day, she'd fulfilled all the requirements. It was as simple as that. The judging for optional routines called for a mandatory completion of a number of required fundamental gymnastics skills, which Nadia accomplished summarily, and additional effort in three distinct areas of "extra credit." These were defined, officially, as *Risk, Originality, and Virtuosity*. If a gymnast performed all the basic requirements without flaw, the maximum score possible was 9.4. If, beyond the fundamentals, you added skills that required Risk you could get up to an additional two tenths of a point added to your score. If you added skills that demonstrated Originality you could get up to two tenths of a point more. And if you performed all of this with Virtuosity you could get another two tenths of a point. Put it all together and you could score the maximum, a 10.

Theoretically.

That scoring system, cursed by more than one gymnast in its time, was called R.O.V.—standing, of course, for Risk, Originality, Virtuosity.

Good gymnasts pulled off all the fundamentals. Great gymnasts pulled off all the fundamentals and then added to their routines equal parts R.O.V. Something Risky. Something Original. Something with Virtuosity.

In recent years gymnastics has gone away from R.O.V. scoring. Maybe it's because the word "risk" makes too many lawyers nervous, but current rules call for an A,B,C,D,E scoring system, where all skills are assigned a specific grade based on difficulty.

To get a 10 a gymnast today must supply the requisite number of skills in each category, A through E.

Personally, for reasons that will become obvious in the chapters to follow, I have never been in favor of the scoring change. I competed for twelve years under the R.O.V. system and I believe it to be a superior scoring system that gets the most out of gymnasts. I saw it consistently inspire competitors at all levels to be the best they could be. I know it was very, very good for—and to—me.

Beyond that, since my last competitive performance as a gymnast in the Los Angeles Olympic Games of 1984, I've been pleased to discover that those three components of risk, originality and virtuosity need not be restricted only to those who do backflips and iron crosses and salute head judges. Understanding and applying the values of R.O.V. can fuel drives toward countless pursuits of perfection. They can—and should—be applied to dreams and goals in all walks of life for all kinds of people. They're the values that were utilized by the British knights already mentioned, Sirs Bannister and Hillary, as well as by Nadia Comaneci. They are universal components when it comes to pursuits of perfection, and the good news is, they are available to us all.

What works for a gymrat can work for anyone!

It is possible, and can be most advantageous, to apply risk, originality and virtuosity every day, in everything we do.

They are what push us to 10's.

In the pages that follow, my purpose is to show how we can all effectively use risk, originality, and virtuosity as we pursue the 10's of our own choosing. No matter what our interests and goals might be, and no matter in what arenas we might perform, there is an uncomplicated formula we can all follow.

In Part I, we will look at the importance of laying down a firm foundation that enables success.

Part II looks at the importance of taking responsible, calculated risks.

Part III looks at the importance of originality.

Part IV looks at the importance of performing with virtuosity.

Part V is the "Do It" section, where, through a variety of examples, we will look at the reality of applying risk, originality and virtuosity in our lives.

In the end, the message that I hope comes across loud and clear—and it's the same message I hope to leave every time address the world's top corporations—is that by adding risk, originality and virtuosity to our lives we can add a good deal of enjoyment to whatever it is we're trying to accomplish. Not only is it a way to improved results, but it's a way to better enjoy the trip.

About that 1976 Olympic routine of Nadia's on the uneven bars. The first "10." Did she deserve it? How great was it? Was it flawless? Well, within the context of what she was doing, it definitely *was* a 10. There was no question that Nadia satisfied all the requirements. She had maximum risk, she had maximum originality, she had maximum virtuosity, and underneath all of that was a solid foundation of gymnastics training that got her to the Olympic Games in the first place. It's why she could stand proud and straight upon dismounting, all 59 inches of her, and smile slyly at the crowd and, especially, at the judges. She'd stumped them, and the thing is, if you go back and look at the tapes, you can see that she knew it. And so did they.

But was it really perfect? Naw. It was done by a human, wasn't it? If the truth be known, Bo Derek probably isn't perfect, either.

Part I

Setting the Stage

I DON'T KNOW WHO WAS MORE EXCITED, WE OR THE POLICE.

My teammates and I had just won the men's Olympic gymnastics team gold medal—the first team title for the United States since the 1904 Olympic Games held in St. Louis, when the gymnastics competition included rope climbing, club swinging, the long jump, and the shot put; and also when *every* team entered was from the United States (decent odds, huh?). In the eighty years since 1904, it would be fair to say that U.S. men's gymnastics had experienced something of a chronic Olympic slump. There had been a grand total of five individual gold medals won, all in the 1932 Games held in Los Angeles, and three of those gold medals were in events that had since been discontinued. The thinking seemed to be, if the Americans could win them, let's cut them out.

Since those '32 Games, just one individual medal—a bronze, won in floor exercise by Peter Kormann in 1976—had been captured by a U.S. male gymnast. Other than that, it had been a very quiet eight decades. The best a U.S. men's team could do was fifth place in the Rome Olympics in 1960. (Subsequent to the '84 Olympics we have had two more medals: Jair Lynch's silver on parallel bars in '96, and Trent Dimas's spectacular gold on horizontal bar in '92.)

Then along came 1984, the Games of L.A., the finals in Pauley Pavilion on the campus at UCLA (my alma mater!), the parallel bars firmly planted on American soil, and topsy suddenly went turvy. The team from the United States made either a comeback or a debut, depending on your sense of history, by beating the reigning world champions and most recent dictators of the sport, the Chinese, and the former perennial dictators of the sport, the Japanese—whose teams wound up wearing silver and bronze, respectively.

Our first-place finish took most of the hometown crowd at Pauley by surprise. They knew we'd won a medal when we were among the three teams that marched out for the medals ceremony at the end of the competition. But since we were sandwiched between the Japanese, who were walking just in front of us, and the Chinese, walking just behind, they didn't guess that medal was gold. Scoring in gymnastics isn't the easiest to decipher, particularly in the team competition when the lowest team member's score is dropped from each of six events, and, let's face it, not everyone in the sellout crowd of more than twelve thousand was a subscriber to *International Gymnast*. I'd say the makeup was about three thousand hardcore gymnastics fans, who had a pretty good idea what was going on, and the rest were Americans who had either drawn out gymnastics tickets in the lottery or were corporate guests of IBM or AT&T or American Express and knew as much about gymnastics as they did about synchronized swimming.

And, too, remember that this was early in the Games of 1984. For reasons that were no doubt tied into the success record of the past eighty years, men's gymnastics was not one of those sports the L.A. organizers had saved until the latter stages of the

Games. Traditionally, host countries like to save what they think will be their best for last—as the Australians did with swimming and diving in 1960, or the Finns with distance running in 1952, for a couple of examples—and in 1984, the Los Angeles organizers chose to save other sports (read: safer bets) for the end of the parade. We were at the front. We took the stage well before the American dominance that would characterize those Games had a chance to become apparent. When we went through our routines, Carl Lewis, who would win four gold medals on the track, hadn't even taken off his sweats yet. Except for compulsories, neither had Mary Lou Retton, the woman gymnast destined to become these Games's darling. When we marched to the medals stand flanked by the Chinese and the Japanese, very few medals had been awarded to anybody, and almost none of the record 174 medals that would go to U.S. athletes. The sight of Americans struggling to choke back tears as the national anthem was played and the Stars and Stripes were raised wasn't common, not yet.

The point is, nobody expected us to win, even if we were from the host nation. We certainly weren't the pre-meet favorite. In the last world championships, held just seven months previous in Budapest, Hungary, we'd finished fourth with the same lineup. Behind the Chinese and the Soviets and the Japanese. When the Olympics rolled around, nobody was holding their breath for the U.S.A. to win. Place, maybe, but not win.

So when we started climbing the steps of the medals podium and didn't stop until we got to the top step, well, the patrons of Pauley Pavilion, collectively realizing for the first time we were on top of the world, no matter if, until that day, many of them had never even *seen* a gymnastics meet, went stark-raving berserk!

The roar was deafening. There may be no fervor like we-beat-the-world fervor. Especially on your home court. We saw it later in Atlanta, then more recently in Salt Lake City. When people ask me what it was like, I say, well, imagine a rock concert and the last day of school rolled into one. The crowd stood and waved American flags and shouted and screamed. Despite the short notice, everyone did a terrific impromptu job of reveling in the triumph. Everyone there really, as the sportscasters say, *stepped up*. From an athlete's perspective, I can tell you, trite as it sounds, that this truly was *The Moment* you dream of. *The Moment* you win the Olympic gold medal and stand at attention while they play the anthem and then everything and everyone goes crazy. *The Moment* you'll never forget. I know I haven't yet. And the thing is, it was just as I'd dreamed it would be, only perhaps even better and certainly crazier. I turned to Bart Conner, who was standing next to me, and told him I was hyperventilating and was afraid I was going to pass out right there on the top step—just drop.

"Just take deep breaths," Bart shouted above the roar, "and don't."

A short and very loud press conference followed, after which we—the members of Team America, sudden celebrities, overnight sensations—were rushed to a van waiting outside, its motor running, because ABC wanted us for that night's nationally televised Olympic wrap-up, LIVE! NOW! . . . And that's where the police came in.

There were four patrol cars, lights flashing, sirens blaring, and sixteen motorcycle cops—our escorts to the ABC studios in Hollywood about ten miles across town on Sunset Boulevard.

We screamed down Sunset at seventy miles an hour, minimum, and didn't stop until we pulled up in front of the studio, where the policemen, wearing these huge smiles, stood by their motorcycles with bugs in their teeth and said "Congratulations guys, and thanks!" Christmas had come in July for them too. To get through traffic they got to do their funeral procession thing, where they'd stop and block traffic and then we'd go through in the van and then they'd have to catch us, pass us, and get to the next intersection to stop traffic, and to do that they had to ride fast! They'd been able to go a hundred miles an hour down Sunset and that didn't happen very often with no one shooting at them.

You can ask us or you can ask those officers. It was a good night all around.

Mr. Mako

While flying down Sunset I took off my gold medal and gave it away.

"Here," I said to my coach, "you take it home for your family to see."

Makoto Sakamoto and I had been together for the past twelve years, as inseparable as smog and Los Angeles, and if there was one thing I knew, I knew that if it hadn't been for Coach Sakamoto, who was and always will be "Mr. Mako" to me, ABC Sports would never have wanted to talk to Peter Vidmar.

We lived what has since been called a "Karate Kid" existence, and I'd have to say that comparison is not far off. Ours was a relationship that went far beyond just coaching and training. I trusted Mr. Mako totally. When he'd say vault I'd ask how high.

If it had happened to anyone else there's a good chance I wouldn't believe it.

But it happened to me, and all because in the fall of 1972, when I was eleven, my mom and I answered a newspaper ad that appeared in the *Santa Monica Evening Outlook:*

FUTURE GYMNASTS GET AID IN CULVER

This weekend, the Culver City Dept. of Parks & Recreation will hold the first experimental gymnastics program designed to develop future Olympic champions. Selection will be made from boys 10–13. No experience necessary. Founder of the program is international gymnastics champion Makoto Sakamoto. Only five boys will be chosen to train under Coach Sakamoto. Tryouts and selection at 11 A.M. at Culver City Jr. High Girls Gym.

My father, John Vidmar, saw the short article as he was reading the newspaper one evening after work. He'd finished the *Los Angeles Times*, which he always read first, and was following up with the local paper—we lived in Ladera Heights, a Los Angeles suburb bordered by Culver City on the north, Inglewood on the south, and Santa Monica on the northwest—when the word "gymnast" caught his eye. Being a former gymnast himself (at L.A.'s Dorsey High School) and knowing that his youngest son, me, had inherited a penchant for jumping off things, he did what most fathers would do in this kind of situation.

"Hey, Doris," he called to my mother in the kitchen. "You should take Pete to this."

Doris Vidmar, my mother and as on top of things as Radar O'Riley on his best day, needed no further prodding. She read the article, asked me if I was interested, I said yes, and if there was one thing in the world that was an absolute certainty after that it was this: We would be at the Culver City Junior High girls gym on the appointed Saturday at 11 A.M. Sharp. For my mom, punctuality was right up there with Godliness, keeping your room straight, and eating your vegetables (she was a dietician).

I met all of the requirements specified in the newspaper. I was 11 years old. I was a boy. And I had no experience. I was 4' 9", 69 pounds after a big dinner, and weak as a frog. I was wearing a Dodgers jacket when, accompanied by my mom, I met the international gymnastics champion Mr. Makoto Sakamoto the following Saturday morning—and signed up to be an "Olympic champion."

Mr. Sakamoto wasn't exaggerating about the international champion part. He was the real deal. Just two months before I met him he'd concluded a fifteen-year competitive career at the

1972 Olympic Games in Munich, and he certainly hadn't let himself go yet. He was 26 years old at the time, 5′ 2″, 125 pounds, and there wasn't a single ounce of fat detectable on his body.

Mr. Mako's goal was simple: Now that he was through competing he wanted to transfer what he had learned to others—to "future Olympic champions" as his ad had specified. Sounded good to me.

He certainly had the learning to impart. He'd been there, done that. Born in Shanghai to Japanese parents, his roots came from a dentist father who'd been wiped out by wartime, not once but twice, and who eventually located on the other side of the Pacific, in Los Angeles, where he raised a family of five and a genuine Japanese garden in the heart of Baldwin Hills, an L.A. suburb to the southwest of downtown. Short, compact, and naturally strong, all the Sakamoto boys did gymnastics. Mako, the youngest, was the best. Trained by his brother, Isamu, he became a United States national champion by the age of 16 and in 1964, at the age of 18, he competed for the United States in the Tokyo Olympic Games, placing in the top 20 overall and first among the Americans.

He won seven national championships in all. As a college gymnast, he was an NCAA champion at USC and also, just for the variety of it, attended Waseda University in Japan and competed in that country's national collegiate championships. For more than a decade he was easily one of the top ten or fifteen gymnasts in the world. If not for the unfortunte timing of a biceps muscle he tore just three weeks before his final Olympics in Munich, he might have medaled in the Games of 1972, instead of just retiring.

He'd tried to go "straight" after the Olympics. He'd taken a job with an import-export firm and after that he'd gone to work for a bank. But none of it fit him like a gym fit him. Makoto Sakamoto had the same kind of feeling for gymnastics that George Patton had for battle. If he wasn't going to compete any longer, well, he still had to do *something* to stay in the arena. He placed the announcement in the newspaper and was back in business.

Although he was only fifteen years older than me, his roots traced back to a gymnastics time in America that was far simpler. He'd never had a coach to teach him the basics. He and his brothers were self-taught out of books they checked out of the library and read in the playground, after which they'd act out the diagrams. They went a step *below* grass roots. When he read about gymnasts using "chalk" on the high bar, Mako went to the store, bought chalkboard chalk, ground up the sticks into powder, put it on his hands, grabbed the playground high bar, swung around, and peeled right off the bar onto his back. It's not the same kind of chalk!

When Mako competed in the Olympic trials as late as 1972 the competition was held in a high school gym and virtually no one was in the seats watching. There were certainly no television cameras there. In 1964, when Mako first won the trials, the U.S. Olympic Committee named his high school gymnastics coach as the head coach of the Olympic team. True story. Just like that, the Los Angeles High School gymnastics coach became the United States' national team coach—because he "coached" Mako.

Obviously, Mako was a self-motivator, and the motivation didn't come from dreams of being rich or famous. Simply being in the gym was enough for him. He didn't like to train, he *loved* to train. (And still does, for that matter. He was recently written up in *USA Today* for doing 160 handstand push-ups on the parallel bars . . . at age 52!)

For Mr. Mako, money and glory never had anything to do with gymnastics. Later on, when I attended UCLA and Mako was hired there as an assistant coach, he didn't even draw a salary for the first couple of years. All he got was a scholarship, which he used to obtain a masters degree in Oriental languages. He made money on the side by translating business journals from English to Japanese. He would finish coaching late at night, drive home, and then translate until 3:00 or 4:00 in the morning, get a few hours' sleep, wake up, and coach gymnastics.

He was not a material man. For Mako, material things were just a necessary nuisance. For the entire twelve years we trained together he drove the same car, very slowly. He'd drive forty-five miles an hour down the San Diego freeway. (He used to say, "Pete, my record speaks for itself. I've never been in an accident." And I'd say "Yeah, but what about all the ones you've caused?") And fashion to him was wearing whatever the latest gymnastics supplier gave you. I've rarely seen him wearing anything that doesn't have a logo on it.

He just never was one for worrying about amenities—or about economics. Back in the '70's, at his "Experimental Gymnastics Program" for the Culver City Department of Parks & Recreation, he got the use of the girl's gym only at night, and he charged his students twenty dollars a month.

Basically, he lived the no-frills life of one with a single-mindedness that was almost monk like in its devotion. They just don't make a whole lot of Mako Sakamotos. He had great peace then, and still does. And, could he coach!

Trust

I handed the gold medal to Mako—he was an assistant coach to U.S. Olympic team head coach Abe Grossfeld—because in the midst of the gold medal euphoria (and no doubt *because* of it) I knew there was no way I'd have gotten there without him. In the end, especially, I realized just how important it was that I'd been raised right, so to speak, gymnastics-wise. I'd had a coach who had systematically taken the time to teach me the fundamentals of my sport, and that in turn had given me a platform to add whatever I could within the natural constraints of my training and physical capabilities. In other words, having the right kind of coaching is what got me to the point where I could concentrate on the risk, originality, and virtuosity part of my sport. Without the proper foundation and fundamentals, I'd have never even *approached* a 10. I needed someone to teach me how to get me to the precipice of perfection.

To my way of thinking, at the very least, the man who had "raised me right" deserved to hang on to that gold medal (although not forever; I got the medal back the next day so I could give it to my future children. Little did I know at the time I should have won five medals).

Over time I'd developed trust in Mako, and it was that trust that allowed me not just to develop my gymnastics skills, but my own self-confidence as well. He made it so I could believe in myself.

With Mr Mako, there just wasn't any question. If he said I was ready, I was ready. My personal thoughts on the subject were immaterial. He would never ask me to try something unless he knew I could do it. Over time I realized that, and became comfortable with it.

A gymnast needs that trust. *Everyone* needs that trust. Someone to believe in you and tell you honestly when you're ready for new heights.

I've got many of examples of Mako telling me I was ready— most times when I still didn't have a clue where I stood, or that I *was* ready.

If it was up to me, for example, I might *never* have opted to do my first double back flip off the high bar.

You may know how it is when you're learning something new. There's always going to be that moment of truth. You've built up to doing it, and up, and up, and then there's the day you go for it—the day your coach tells you to.

Back in the Culver City girls' gym, we had a routine that we followed every day without fail. All the gymnasts would walk in and line up in front of Mako and he'd say some short greeting like "OK, let's have a good workout today," followed by "Open workout!," which was our cue to clap our hands to our side. That clap meant that from that moment on you did gymnastics and nothing else. You didn't think about school or your girlfriend or what you were going to do that night after practice. You didn't horse around. You thought about your training, period. When you clapped your hands to your side everything else was gone. That was the idea. If you ever watch Japanese gymnasts at a competition you'll see them clap their hands to their side. To me it's their way to focus. When you finish your workout you do the same thing—clap—and now it's OK to think about other things. Kind of like going into and out of hypnosis.

Well, one day, right after he said "Open workout!" and we clapped our hands, Mako turned to me and almost as an aside said, "Oh, and Pete, today I want you to do double back on high bar."

Double back on high bar!
The dreaded double back.

I spent a lot of time that day in the bathroom. I was using the age-old ploy—if they're looking for you and someone says "I think he's in the bathroom," maybe after a while they'll forget about you. But it didn't work. When I came out of the bathroom, Mr. Mako was there, waiting.

Eventually I found myself on the high bar, about to attempt my first-ever double back flip. It's a basic, but nonetheless scary skill that calls for you to release the bar when you've got a lot of momentum and then execute a double back flip as gravity whips you toward the mat, nine feet or so below. We didn't have a spotting belt in our gym (with ropes on pulleys attached to the ceiling). Nowadays, most young gymnasts have spotting belts as well as landing pits filled with cubes of foam rubber.

Well, I jumped up to the bar. The other kids in the gym could see the shaking of my arms. I performed some giant swings, and let go of the bar, fortunately at the right time. I was so nervous I over-rotated completely (trust is one thing; nerves are another).

My feet never touched the mat. I went so far that I landed on my back. Wham! But I'd done it. Well, overdone it. I got up and said "Yes!"

So he was right—I *was* ready.

Experiences like that constantly increased my trust in my coaching, as well as my confidence. I knew Mako wouldn't have me try anything until he was confident I could do it. His confidence gave me confidence. Gymnastics was rewarding and fun. I was always wondering what I was going to do next.

Of course there were times I'd think Mako was going too far, even if he never did. The one day I was convinced he was going too fast too soon was the first day he had me try a double back flip on the floor.

Now, a double back flip off the high bar is one thing. The high bar is nine feet above the ground and you have all that distance to do your rotations. But a double back off the floor means you create your own height and distance, depending on the momentum you get when you spring off the mat. A double back flip requires a lot of spring.

Mako's older brother, Mickey, happened to visit the gym the day Mako decided I would debut a double back off the floor. That made me suspicious. I wondered if the only reason he wanted me to try it was because he wanted to impress his brother.

I had reason to be nervous. For one thing, the Culver City junior high girl's gym wasn't exactly the Taj Mahal of gyms. All of our equipment was stored in closets against the wall and was only brought out at night for our workouts. We used these vinyl-covered foam mats that were only about two inches thick. At the end of the mats was an eight-inch thick mat that served as our landing area. Underneath it all was the hardwood gym floor. It wasn't really any different from jumping off the highway with two inches of cushion.

For another thing, my legs were not what you'd call my strong point. My nickname in the gym wasn't "horse" or "tiger"

—it was "chicken legs." There were people in the gym with bigger arms than my legs. When I was eleven, I actually went to a novelty shop and bought a pair of gag socks that looked like chicken legs—on the theory that it's always a good idea to make fun of yourself before somebody else does it first.

And for one more thing, I had a coach who, in spite of all his fine qualities, was not what you would call a master spotter. A spotter's job is to be in exactly the right place to be able to catch you or correct your positioning before you do something harmful to yourself, such as crash. At UCLA we used to say Mako had two spots: The "eye spot" (watching the crash) and the "You OK?" spot (after the crash). After executing both these "spots" he'd invariably say, "Looked good to me, go do it again."

So when Mako, with his older brother looking on, moved to the middle of the mat and said, "I'll spot you," I raised my left eyebrow. I wondered if this wasn't finally the time when I was being asked to do something for which I truly wasn't ready.

I started running before I had a chance to over-analyze all of this. Mako had taught me to never do anything halfway in gymnastics. Halfway, he used to say, is an invitation to injury. If you're going to go for it, then go for it, all out, so I went for it, looking like Carl Lewis sprinting down the long jump ramp. I was flying, and before I knew it I'd gone into a back handspring that gave me more pop and more momentum than I'd ever felt before. I clasped my hands around my knees as I went up and was sure they were going to slip off because of all the centrifugal force I was generating. Then as I was going around and around I felt these sudden jolts to my body—bam! bam! bam!—which was the poor job of spotting by Mako. After that, all of a sudden, boom! impact! I did a three-point landing, not exactly the landing of choice for a double back flip. More or less simultaneously, I lit on knee, knee, and face. I hit so hard on my right knee that to this day I can scratch the top of it and not feel anything.

Mako was right there . . . on top of me.

"Allriiiight!" he said. "You did it! You didn't even need a spot! Now go do it again!"

Roots

My father's greatest dismount was when he landed on his feet out of the polio ward.

He was 29 years old and I wasn't born yet when they diagnosed the polio. What FDR had, he had.

It was the early 1950's. The country was still recovering from the second World War, and John Vidmar felt he was a fortunate man. He had a good job and was rising through the ranks as a sales rep with the Byron Jackson Pump Company of Los Angeles. He had two college degrees—a bachelors degree in mechanical engineering from Cal-Berkeley and a masters degree from that other school across town from UCLA (USC). And he had a young, growing family. He and Doris, my mom, had already had my three oldest brothers and sisters, with plans for more.

But then one workday when my dad stopped for lunch between appointments, he noticed he was having trouble swallowing his food. After lunch, he stopped by the doctor's office on the way to a business appointment scheduled for later that afternoon.

The doctor, who spotted the polio symptoms immediately, told my dad he had to get to the hospital, to which he replied that he couldn't possibly do that, he had an appointment he couldn't afford to miss. He had a *job*.

"John," the doctor said, "you don't understand."

Forty-eight hours later he lay in the hospital—paralyzed.

Polio would hit like that, in an instant, after the barest of warning signs. Luckily my father made it to the hospital, where they did what they could for him, which in the '50's, before Dr. Jonas Salk and his miracle vaccine, consisted chiefly of soaking your muscle cramps with hot towels.

He was in a ward with forty other people, all but two of them young children—polio's usual victims. A man who only days earlier had been a picture of healthy perpetual motion was now confined to dining every night through a straw. Patience suddenly became a virtue without an option. Polio—a disease so cruel that it doesn't let you move but still lets you feel—demands it of you. All you can do is wait. Day after day, week after week, my dad lay there, his life in the balance, hoping the virus *poliomyelitis* would run its course and somehow spare him the kind of destruction you can't repair.

As he lay there his main thought was about what this was doing to his young family. It was that concern, he said later, more than any other, that heightened his determination to see this thing through. He needed to get back out on the road and make sales and *provide for his family*.

And that's exactly what he did. They came close to putting him in an iron lung when his breathing got so labored that it appeared he would no longer be able to get enough oxygen on his own. At one point a doctor actually sent out a call for the dreaded machine that would make the body so dependent that it could never be removed. But then bad fortune turned to good. His breathing got better, not worse, and the virus disappeared, its exit every bit as abrupt as its entrance. Those who had been fervently praying—including my dad; that was the one thing he *could* do—saw it as a miracle.

It left him with a permanently atrophied left leg that never would get much bigger than a No. 2 pencil. It also left him without a deltoid muscle in one arm and without a triceps muscle in the other arm. But it left him, that was the main thing, and when he got out of the hospital he hit the sidewalk—figuratively, at least—running. There were months of rehabilitation at home to come. Hundreds of baths using a crane and pulley system. Thousands of hours re-training all the muscles that could still be re-trained. But as soon as it was humanly possible, John Vidmar was back making his rounds, back climbing the corporate ladder. He eventually progressed from sales rep to senior vice president in charge of all international operations for what became the largest pump company in the world.

Family Values

Given that background, you'll understand why it was fruitless for any of his children to argue with John Vidmar's family motto: *Vidmars Don't Quit.*

That was the basic extent of his philosophy. He was not a driving or domineering parent, and neither was my mother. All of their children—there would be six of us in all, including a brother who died at 13 of a congenitive heart problem—were free to choose our own paths. I have one brother, John, who got a masters degree in art and is now an executive for a large welding supplies company. My other brother, Tom, graduated in engineering, got an MBA, and is the vice president of a computer parts manufacturer. My sister Melissa was the only female engineering student at Brigham Young University when she enrolled there in the '60's. And my sister Dodie became a teacher specializing in working with the learning disabled. Me, I'm a talking gymnast. We all chose our own directions. We all went our own way. The only thing we weren't allowed to choose was to quit something we started.

There was certainly no concerted effort for me to be a gymnast. I was the first of the children in the family to even try the sport. My older brothers' sports of choice were wrestling and surfing. My father had competed in gymnastics in high school and his brother, my uncle Dick Vidmar, was the conference floor exercise champion at USC in the 1950's, so there was definitely a gymnastics heritage in the family—although until I came along, no one chose to pick up on it. My dad used to hang around Ocean Park, near Venice Beach, back in the days when it was known as Muscle Beach—a favorite hangout of L.A.-area gymnasts (Joe Gold, of Gold's Gym, and the original Fitness Guru, Jack Lallane, used to hang out there) who would lift weights and show off by doing handstands and various flips and jumps. My dad used to climb to the top of buildings next to the beach and do handstands on the top while a buddy of his would walk among the tourists and ask for money. He has some great stories of those Depression-era days.

At 5′ 4″, he had the compact frame of a gymnast, although that would prove to be something of a problem when World War Two broke out. On December 8, 1941, the day after the attack on Pearl Harbor, my dad went to a recruiting office in San Francisco to enlist (it was a different world back then). They turned him down, twice, on account of his height. After the second try he remembers sitting on the steps outside of the navy recruiting center, in tears. An officer walked by and asked him what was wrong. "They won't let me in the navy," my dad said, and the officer said, "Well *I'll* let you in the navy" and he pulled rank and did just that.

It was a good thing John Vidmar got in the navy because that got him to upstate New York, where he attended submarine and engineering officers' school, and where he met Doris Neely, a graduate student at the time at nearby Cornell University. They fell in love, were soon married, and after the war they settled in Los Angeles.

My mother, who got her degree in dietetics, lived this incredibly orderly life that said that you *always* played by the rules. Her kids didn't miss school, for one example. You had to be on your death bed to miss school. She believed if you'd made a commitment then you should be there and you should be there on time. No excuses. No alibis. A "Just Do It" kind of mom well before the slogan became famous. She was the best.

Both my mother and my father were completely supportive of whatever their children were pursuing. But it wasn't a vicarious kind of thing with them. They had their own lives. They did-n't live through their children. But if you chose it, they were be-hind you. I don't think they missed any competition I was ever in. I was the youngest and by that time they could afford to travel, and with no kids left at home they had more time to do just that. They really enjoyed it. But I remember my dad asking me once, around the time I was entering college, why I was doing gymnastics. "It's not just to please your mother and me, is it?" he asked. He really wanted to know. If that was the case, he didn't want me to continue. I told him no, I was doing it for me. It was an answer that pleased both of us. What mattered to my dad and my mom was that my interests were my interests, my passions were my passions, not theirs. My independence was im-portant to them.

So I had these supportive, committed parents who'd grown up during the Depression and the war and survived polio and endured the loss of a son and insisted that not only would you finish what you started, but you'd choose what it was going to be, and you'd do it *on time* . . .

. . . and then these people introduced me to Mako Sakomoto.

I didn't have much choice other than to be committed, inde-pendent, and on time myself.

Chemistry

Unlike most Americans—OK, almost *all* Americans—the mem-bers of the 1984 U.S. Olympic gymnastics team were not sur-prised to be among the medal contenders in the Los Angeles Games. Maybe the United States had never exactly been the Dream Team of world gymnastics, but even if we were all but anonymous, we knew we had still been a few places and done a few things.

At the 1979 world championships in Fort Worth, Texas, a U.S. team that included half of the members on the '84 Olympic team, myself included, had placed third, behind only the Soviet Union and Japan. In the 1983 world championships, held in Budapest, Hungary, just seven months before the L.A. Games, what was exactly the American Olympic team placed fourth, just one spot out of the medals, behind China, Japan and the Soviet Union.

Actually, the 1980 team selected to compete in the Moscow Olympics just might have won the United States its first modern-day team gymnastics medal four years previous. You never know. And you never will know, because President Carter's boycott prevented that squad from ever chalking up. One of our team members, Ron Galimore, was the first African American to make a U.S. Olympic gymnastics team. He was probably the finest vaulter in the world. He frequently scored 10's. I believe he could have made history in Moscow. I was as disappointed for him as I was for probably any other athlete that was denied a chance to compete at those Games. (Sixteen years later in Atlanta, Jair Lynch of Stanford became the country's first male African American medalist in gymnastics, taking the silver on the parallel bars).

Three members of the '84 team, including me, were holdovers from 1980, and I don't think any of us—or any of the other American Olympians from 1980, for that matter—would minimize the impact the four-year wait had in heightening our resolve to perform well in the Olympics if we ever got the chance again.

We were as ready as we were ever going to be in 1984, that was our feeling, and when you threw in the fact that the Games would be staged in Los Angeles, U.S.A., just up the freeway from Disneyland and just down the freeway from the HOLLYWOOD sign, in front of all those red-white-and-blue flags, it added up to an ideal location. The right place at the right time. We had the home-country advantage.

Going in, we had an excellent attitude, which never hurts; and, as it turned out, we also had the stuff of every coaches' dream: good chemistry.

Because of the unusual nature of gymnastics as a team sport, the right chemistry may be as important for a gymnastics team as it is for any other sports team. There aren't too many other sports where you compete *against* your teammates at the exact same time you're competing *with* them. But that's how it is in gymnastics. It's kind of like the six of you are trying to carry nitroglycerin *together* while you're also all going your separate ways.

Team gymnastics is a tricky business. At the same time you and your teammates are setting your sights on the team trophy, you also have to each focus on your personal results in the individual all-around competition. Paranoia runs rampant in gymnastics meets for good reason. Hey, everyone *is* after you.

To be a good team member, a gymnast needs the heart of an assassin AND a diplomat. Not the easiest of combinations. Luckily, in '84, I had teammates who had big hearts.

We tended to feed on each other rather than off each other. One person's strength became everyone's strength. We covered each other's weaknesses. As a result, the whole far exceeded the sum total of the parts. It's the best team of which I've ever been a part.

I remember just before the Olympics began when we were leaving a team training session in Los Angeles and stopped to look back at the defending world champion Chinese team, now working out.

"We can beat those guys," said Jim Hartung, who was from Nebraska, where you said what you thought.

My neck swiveled when he said that. All we needed was a member of the media overhearing us and carrying that quote to the front page of the next morning's *Los Angeles Times*. The last thing we wanted was to provide the Chinese with something they could paste to their locker room wall (and then bring in a translater who would read it to them).

Fortunately, nobody heard what Jim said except us, and that was good because it was amazing the impact that statement had—

at least on me. I knew what he meant and I knew he was not being cocky, he was being honest. He sensed what we all sensed—that we were capable! I was glad that he said it out loud. It was a figurative breaking of the ice for me. My teammate had said something that I was thinking silently, something that I think we were all thinking silently: The world champions *were* beatable. They were good, sure, but they weren't gods. They did their dismounts two legs at a time, same as us. Looking back, I realize how important it was for us to understand that going in. Because if we didn't think it first, I'm not sure we could have competed with them.

In one way or another, on and off the mats, every man on that team took a turn in doing something that was inspiring and positive to everyone else.

Curiously, it wasn't a team that at first glance made you think "instant success." One thing that could have been a problem but wasn't, was a natural division that cut along college lines. Half the team—Tim Daggett, Mitch Gaylord and I—had competed in college at UCLA, and the other half was from the heartland—Scott Johnson and Jim Hartung had competed for Nebraska and Bart Conner at Oklahoma. On and off for the past four years, then, we had all spent considerable energy trying to defeat each other at any number of collegiate meets. Now, the West was meeting the Midwest. Our familiarity with each other could have either bred contempt or respect. We were lucky. We wound up liking *and* respecting each other.

The Team

On most of the events, Scott Johnson was our leadoff man, a.k.a. the sacrificial lamb. Every gymnastics team needs somebody who will go first and, in effect, sacrifice their personal ambitions for the good of the team. The key is to have a leadoff man who will immediately set a high standard. The traditional psychology of gymnastics judging calls for judges to start with lower marks and work up to higher ones—the theory of the judges being that the team is going to save its best for last, and if they start their judging too high they won't have any room to reward the later gymnasts. It's not a perfect system, and it seems like they're always making changes trying to make the system more equitable. But the reality in any sport that uses subjective judging is that you're going to have to deal with the nuances and peculiarities of the judging. In gymnastics, there are plenty of nuances and peculiarities.

What we wanted in 1984 was a leadoff man so good that the competition would begin with a high common denominator. *A high tide raises all ships* kind of mentality. As our leadoff hitter at the Olympics, Scott raised the floor, so to speak. He was the youngest member of the team. A lot of his best gymnastics was ahead of him (Scott's all-around championship at the U.S. Nationals three years later, in 1987, was the latest national title won by a member of that 1984 team and completed a teamwide sweep of a trophy that Bart Conner won in 1975 and 1979, I won in 1980 and 1982, Jim Hartung won in 1981, Mitch Gaylord won in 1983 and 1984 and Tim Daggett won in 1986—as strong an indicator as any that the team of '84 was solid from top to bottom).

Scott's tenacity was pure inspiration for all of us. He had this fearlessness about him that was contagious. He never ate a calorie he didn't burn *immediately*. He was a human superball, always bouncing off the walls. Just before the 1983 world championships before a tune-up meet in France he made that literal. He was working on the trampoline, which was positioned next to a wall of the gym. Mitch Gaylord double-bounced him (by jumping on the trampoline just before Scott hits it, to tighten the tramp, and give Scott an extra few feet of air). Scott went flying at the wrong angle and did a double twisting double flip that ended with his face against one of that rough plaster cottage-cheese wall. When he bounced off that wall, he had blood flooding down his cheek. He went over to the coach and asked for a Band-Aid. (He has no face and he's asking for a Band-Aid!)

Then he grabbed the wet chalk rag and wiped his face with it and got back on the tramp. Scott was tenacious.

Our other Nebraskan, Jim Hartung, came to the national team as the most decorated collegiate gymnast ever. Nebraska won a pair of NCAA team championships with Jim and he was a 22-time individual All-American. I still count as my greatest personal gymnastics moment outside of the Olympics the night in Lincoln, Nebraska, when I was able to edge Jim for the NCAA all-around championship. Not only because of the title, but because of the sight of all those Cornhuskers and Hartung standing in the soldout arena and applauding the enemy from UCLA.

Whereas Scott was hyper, Jim was quiet. He had a great sense of humor—very sarcastic and very dry—and he was the most patriotic man on the team, very much a team player, the kind you'd want to sit next to in a fox hole or a nuclear submarine, let alone the high bar rotation. At the Olympics, as always, he was Mr. Dependability, the backbone of the team. He did not miss one routine. Not one.

Bart Conner was the team's link to the big time. He'd been there and done that. The oldest man on the team, Bart was a couple of years out of college when the Olympics came around. In 1984 he already had signed some TV contracts and in his apartment he had racks full of clothes. I can tell you for a fact that he was the only one of us who owned his own Porsche. The rest of us used to look at his lifestyle in awe, like we were Bart's kid brothers. The '84 team was Bart's third Olympic team. He'd first competed as an Olympian while still in high school in Montreal in 1976—where Nadia Comaneci also made her debut. (Who could have known back then that fourteen years later, after Nadia escaped from the tyranny of Nicolae Ceausescu's Romania and came to America, that those two Montreal Olympians would get married and build a house in Oklahoma?)

Bart was also on the 1980 team that didn't compete, so he was our only three-time Olympian and the only one on our team with actual Olympic experience. He was also very recognizable. It's fair to say that two male gymnasts, Kurt Thomas and Bart Conner, were responsible for making men's gymnastics appealing to television. It was their two-man rivalry in the late '70's that first caught the attention of the networks. Here were two very telegenic, articulate athletes with a flair for competing. To this day, Kurt Thomas remains the most uncanny performer I've ever seen, the kind of competitor who could struggle and struggle with a skill and then, when they turned on the cameras and it was for real, he'd nail it better than anybody. Bart was like that too. He could have all kinds of trouble working out in the gym and then, in the heat of the competition, he'd look as if he were born to do what he was doing. He thrived on pressure. He won the gold medal on parallel bars in Los Angeles with a dismount that was absolutely perfect, and it was a dismount he almost never landed successfully in training.

Bart proved his grit, too, by coming back from a biceps muscle he'd torn at the Chunichi Cup in Japan in late 1983. Talk about bad timing. The Olympics were only a little more than six months away and he suddenly had an arm that wouldn't work. He had an operation immediately and woke up in a hospital with a machine that would constantly bend and strengthen his arm. It seemed he'd barely gotten out of rehab by the time the Olympic trials competition came around. Against the odds he somehow managed to survive those trials and make the team. Not only did his determination inspire the rest of us, but I think that going through what he went through made facing the Chinese a lot less formidable for him.

I met Mitch Gaylord at my very first gymnastics competition. I was twelve and Mako took me to a meet at the L.A. Valley College out in the San Fernando Valley. Mitch was from Coach Dan Connelly's club, California Sun Gymnastics, which was headquartered in the San Fernando Valley. Mako brought my club teammate Bob Kuriyama and me to compete and I remember I finished second on floor and third on vault and Bob finished third on floor and second on vault. Those were the only two events we competed in. I also remember that Mitch won them both. In all, he won five of the meet's six events. When he was just a tiny guy, they were already calling Mitch Gaylord a phenom.

Both of us being L.A. guys, our paths crossed again and again. He had a struggle for a while when he grew about six inches in six months and he had to get used to his new body, but we were destined to be lifelong rivals—friendly rivals, but still rivals. We wound up both signing with UCLA as freshmen, where we put our rivalry to good use. I know I'm a better gymnast for having had Mitch in the gym. I always had my eye on him, watching what he was doing, how he was training, measuring my progress against his progress. Mitch was one of the most physically gifted athletes I've ever seen. He had an air sense like a cat. He just always *knew* where he was. He rarely crashed or fell, and when he did he still made it look good. My crashes, by comparison, were always ugly.

We tended to trade triumphs back and forth. In '83 and '84, for example, the two years leading up the Olympics, he was the national all-around champion both years and I won the all-around at the trials both years. We flip-flopped like that a lot. The competition was definitely good for us.

We were living proof that there is no one "right way" to train. We couldn't have been more opposite if we'd tried. I liked to train slowly and methodically, the way Mako brought me up. Mitch liked to train fast. Just boom! and go! He worked with Mako for a while but it didn't suit him. The pace was too methodical, the workout system too structured. Mitch trained under a few different coaches, including UCLA Head Coach Art Shurlock, Kurt Thomas and finally, Mitch's brother, Chuck. He had to find what worked for him. He couldn't spend six hours in a gym. For him that was counterproductive. At UCLA sometimes we'd try to work out together, but before long I'd look around and he was two events ahead of me.

Mitch was also somewhat of a teen idol. His picture was on the cover of many a teen magazine. He was even on the cover of *Esquire*. After the Olympics, when the team went on a tour of the country, giving exhibitions at a number of arenas across America, there were plenty of teenage groupies who followed us around. At one stop, I think it was Philadelphia, I was warming up during intermission when this huge crowd of teenage girls kept calling out "Peter! Peter!" I acted like I didn't notice but of course I did notice and they kept it up. "Please turn around!" they kept saying and so finally I turned around and they screamed, "Oh, look, he turned around!"

They had this huge bouquet of flowers and they kept motioning for me to come closer, so finally I decided I'd give them their thrill and I walked over to where they were.

"Yes," I said.

"Oh Peter!" they screamed, holding out the flowers. "Give these to Mitch!"

That was Mitch. He had the talent, and the looks.

I first met Tim Daggett, my best friend on and off the team, when as a teenager about to enroll at UCLA he moved from the east to California to train with Mako. He moved into my parent's house and we became fast friends. My oldest son is named after Tim. Tim's son is named Peter. How's that for an obnoxious friendship? We shared many similar interests, including a passion for gymnastics. I was borderline fanatical about the sport and yet sometimes Tim managed to make me look downright apathetic. Most people recognize Tim as the expert gymnastics announcer for NBC Sports. He now runs Daggett's Gold Medal Gymnastics Club in West Springfield, a successful program with over a thousand kids, some of them the top gymnasts in the country.

For five years we trained together, practically daily, and whatever I could I let rub off on me. As a competitor, I can tell you that "Tim" was not short for timidity. Tim Daggett was relentless in his training and in his performing. You name the apparatus, he attacked it. His style was pure aggression. It was that style that caused Gordon Maddox, who was a gymnastics commentator for ABC Sports, to shout out during one of Tim's all-out pommel horse routines at the Olympics, "He's all over that horse like a naked lady!" I cringe as I write this. (It was obviously a much less politically correct time.) All across America that's what they heard about Tim Daggett, "He's all over that horse like a naked lady!" And for a couple of months after that, that's all Tim Daggett heard from his teammates.

Holding this collection of Bruins, Cornhuskers and an Oklahoma Sooner together, more or less, was our head coach, Abraham (Abe) Grossfeld, who I felt was tailor-made for the task. A two-time Olympian himself, in 1956 and 1960, Abe's selection made him a two-time Olympic coach as well, in 1972 and again in 1984. It's possible that he knew every single significant person in gymnastics—personally. Anywhere in the world. He just knew everybody. Officials, judges, competitors. So that was a big help. And since he was neither a Bruin nor a Cornhusker nor a Sooner—for his day job he was the head gymnastics coach at Southern Connecticut State College (now University) in New Haven—he brought an important sense of neutrality to the team. He didn't play favorites. He didn't make concessions for anyone. Subtly and very effectively, he created an atmosphere of camaraderie, not dissension. On a team that wound up having what they call "good chemistry," Abe Grossfeld was the chief chemist.

Looking back, we had a lot more going for us on that team of '84 than just some skilled gymnasts—much more than we realized at the time. We had a strong young leadoff man, we had a worldly veteran, we had guys who relied on finesse and wile, we had guys who relied on strength and aggression, we had rivalries that cemented rather than fragmented, we had the right blend of coaching . . .

. . . And in the end, we had our country's flag raised to the top of the pole.

After we realized we'd outscored the Chinese and the Japanese and it would be us climbing the victory stand to the top step, we had about twenty minutes before the actual medal ceremony. Once again, very few in the crowd that night at Pauley Pavilion were yet clued in that the guys from the United States had won gold. They looked at us celebrating down on the floor as a signal that we'd won *something* and, given the history of U.S. gymnastics, any medal was worth a celebration.

But we knew we'd done what Jim Hartung had suggested we *could* do that day as we looked over our shoulders at the Chinese working out. We knew we had indeed beaten them. And we knew we'd done it together. For me it was like they show sometimes in the movies, when the background gets fuzzy and the focus is on only a few objects right in front of you. All I could really see during those twenty minutes before we took our bows on the winner's podium were my teammates. We high-fived and we hugged and we celebrated together—caught up in the euphoria of realizing we'd done something collectively we never could have done alone. It's twenty minutes I'll never forget.

Foundation

What's become more and more obvious to me as time has gone on is how important it was to be put in a position that made it easy for me—and for the entire '84 team—to go for some risk, some originality, and some virtuosity. For those Olympic Games of 1984 we'd created an atmosphere than enabled us to be as risky, as original, and to employ as much virtuosity, as possible.

The role of parents, coaches, and teammates is incalculable, as is the role of other mentors and role models. Not just in gymnastics, but in any area of life and any pursuit. In business, there is no substitute for strong leaders, for capable teachers, and for supportive co-workers. Those are the businesses that have consistent success, both collectively and individually. In education, in politics, in personal relationships, in athletics, in any area you care to mention, the same rules apply. The importance of stability and support cannot be overemphasized.

I was lucky as a gymnast and I know it. I had a fine combination of parents, coaches, and teammates that provided me with a solid foundation that gave me the opportunity to go as far as I decided I wanted to go. I had to be willing to do my part, of course, but they put me in a position in which I *could* be successful.

I had parents who gave me my independence but insisted that I honor my commitments. I had coaching that kept me focused on things I often didn't even realize I was focusing on. And I had fellow teammates and coaches who pushed, supported and inspired me. It's the risk, originality and virtuosity that gets you from the 9.4 to the 10. But it's the sound fundamentals you're standing on that get you to the 9.4. You don't need to be a mathematician to realize what's by far the biggest part of that number.

Part II

Risk

"He most prevails who nobly dares."

WILLIAM BROOME

"Never tell me the odds!"

HAN SOLO TO C3PO IN STAR WARS

I FELL NINE FEET and that wasn't even close to the worst of it.

The year was 1983, the country was Hungary, the city was Budapest, and the guy who was on foot, miles from his hotel and *not* hailing a cab was me. You could have pulled up in Bart

Conner's Porsche and tossed me the keys and I'd have tossed them back. Sometimes you have to walk. I had to walk.

Just moments before I'd been in the Budapest Sports Arena, going through a routine on the high bar that I thought was going to turn me into a world champion. I was 22 years old at the time and competing in my third world championships—and these weren't just any world championships. With the Olympics coming up in less than eight months in Los Angeles, these "worlds" were serving as a tune-up to those Games, a final preview of upcoming Olympic medalists.

I was in second place going into the high bar finals; close enough to the lead that it wasn't out of the question to think about the world championship possibilities. And I wasn't the only one. Between the preliminaries and the finals, word had spread. Maybe not to every street corner of Budapest, but definitely to the cameras of ABC's *Wide World of Sports*, which were primed to tape the finals. And when the Japanese gymnast who was leading the competition fell during his routine, those cameras focused in on me, Peter Vidmar, United States of America, all set to chronicle my ascent to the top. I was ready too. All I had to do was nail my routine and I would be the new *World Horizontal Bar Champion*. Kind of a neat thing.

The value of the TV cameras was not lost on me. I knew that it was *Wide World of Sports* that had made Kurt Thomas the most famous American gymnast ever. I knew it was Kurt Thomas in the early '70's who forged a reputation as the best "gamer" in gymnastics history. He always saved his best for whenever they turned on the red light. When it counted, in other words.

By using television as a positive, Kurt Thomas had easily done more for U.S. gymnastics than any other American gymnast. He hadn't done too badly by Kurt Thomas, either.

Now was my chance to be the next Kurt Thomas and I knew it. (And so, I suspect, did Kurt Thomas, who, along with Al Michaels, was handling the broadcast that night for ABC.)

There was one slight problem.

I was suddenly having difficulty with a particular skill in my high bar routine—a tricky maneuver that I'd managed to pull off without a hitch in the preliminaries, but now was giving me problems. This was a skill that had gotten me into world championship contention in the first place. Indeed, this was the skill I needed to do if I wanted to get my two-tenths of a point for risk.

But like I said, it was tricky. It called for me to swing around the bar, then let go, fly straight up over the bar into a half turn, straddle my legs, come back down, catch the bar, immediately let go again, do a back flip with a half turn in the pike position, come back down and catch the bar. Trust me, it's hard.

As I warmed up before the finals I kept having problems performing it correctly and, as a result, kept getting more and more frustrated. This was no time for things to go bad.

Of course, worry soon gave way to panic. I remember I looked at my coach and said, "Mako, you've gotta help me. I've got fifteen minutes until the competition starts and I can't do this right! It's my only risky skill! I have to do this! What's wrong?"

Mako watched me.

"Oh, just pike more on your swing," he said.

"Uh, arch more at the bottom."

"Try letting go of the bar a little later."

All these insightful tips, followed by the ultimate coaching wisdom that we've all heard before:

"Just do it right!"

But I wasn't doing it right, and for a fleeting moment I decided I'd just not do it. I'd leave it out. Why not? I wouldn't get the two-tenths of a point for risk, but I could still score as high as a 9.8. A 9.8 is a good score. That should be enough to put me on the victory podium. But I knew it wouldn't be enough to put me *on top* of the victory podium. If I left out that risky skill, I might be able to win the bronze medal. With some luck, maybe even the silver. But I knew, under those circumstances, I couldn't win the gold medal. I knew some other guys in the finals would be taking some chances and at least one of them would be successful with his "big trick" and he would finish on top. Someone else would get the gold medal. I also instinctively knew that it wasn't every day you got a chance to be a world champion—in anything. Now I had that chance—and I was going to play it safe? I was going to throw out the risk now that I was this close?

No! I wasn't. That was my answer. I decided to stick to the game plan. I'd leave that risky skill in. With it, I would ride to the top of the world—or else.

So I marched into the arena with the rest of the finalists. The window of opportunity opened wide in a matter of minutes. The gymnast who was in first place competed before me, and he made a big mistake. All I had to do now was perform my routine successfully, and I would become the World Horizontal Bar Champion. When my name was called I signaled the superior judge and jumped up and grabbed the bar. The risky skill came right at the beginning of the routine so I swung around the bar, let go, came straight up over the bar, did a half turn, straddled my legs, came back down, caught the bar, immediately let go again, did that back flip with the half turn in the pike position, so far so good, came back down to catch the bar . . . and the bar . . .

. . . was

. . . not . . .

. . . there.

That's when gravity, the supreme justice of gymnastics, prevailed.

After dropping nine feet, I hit the mat.

Now, there is a rule that I'm confident everyone knows about my sport: You're only allowed one dismount in a performance.

I did the only thing I could do. I jumped up off the floor, grabbed the bar again, and finished my routine. But I was already history. I landed my "second" dismount perfectly—big deal—saluted the judges, jumped off the platform, grabbed my bags,

and left the arena. I was devastated. Destroyed. Disconsolate. In-
consolable. I'd blown it. I'd choked. I'd failed. I knew it. And I'd
managed to do it on *Wide World of Sports*! My teammates told me
that when Kurt Thomas, in the broadcast booth, saw this
"wannabe" crash and burn he just flipped his pencil in the air in
disappointment.

In researching this book, I still refuse to look up my final placing. I think maybe I placed eighth. And if you're the thinking,
hmm, eighth place in the *world* is not that bad, I thank you. But
there were only eight people in the competition.

It wasn't not being world champion that bothered me the
most. It was that I'd had the opportunity and I hadn't come
through. I hadn't done a Kurt Thomas. And to make things
worse, I honestly thought I would. That's what got to me, that's
what I kept thinking about over and over again as I walked
back to my hotel. *I thought I would come through!* And I hadn't!
Doubts suddenly came creeping in from all corners. Deep down
I wondered if I would ever be able to rise to the occasion under
pressure. Did I have what it takes? When the heat was on and it
came time to do that risky skill, or one just like it, would I always
crack?

Head down, that's what consumed my thoughts as I walked
through the streets of Budapest. It wasn't until I got to the hotel
and was halfway through the front door that Mako and his
brother, Isamu, who also coached me, caught up to me. I didn't
much feel like talking to them but we were in the space between
the hotel's double entry doors, the area that keeps the heat from
getting out and, in this case, was keeping me from getting in.
They had me cornered.

They said a lot of things. But this is what I remember:

"This is not the end."

"Everything is a learning experience," said Mako, "even competition. What you did tonight can be a valuable learning experience. You can benefit from this."

35

Mako didn't know it at the time—because I didn't tell him—but what he said hit a nerve with me. He was right. This was a valuable learning experience. I didn't want to hear that but I knew he was right. That fall taught me something that I somehow hadn't completely learned until that night:

Never—Ever!—take anything for granted.

Especially don't take risks for granted.

I promised myself that from that day forward, if I was going to take risks, I was going to be ready for them.

There would be no more fooling around. I knew that double release move on the high bar was extremely difficult. I was the only person in the world doing it at the time, so that should have been my first clue. I got maximum risk points for it precisely *because* of its difficulty. It was a move that needed extra attention. It wasn't something I could take for granted. But every day in the gym I *had* taken it for granted—by treating it just like the two hundred or so other tricks I had to work on. I'd given it no extra care. And yet I knew it needed it.

The Olympics were less than eight months away. I resolved that from then on, I'd either go back to the high bar at the end of my workouts or stay on the bar longer, and I'd work overtime on that risky double release move. I was determined to learn my lesson. The next time the heat was on, I did not want to fall.

So that's what I did. For the next eight months, there wasn't a workout between Budapest and Los Angeles that didn't include an extra session, or two, working on that high bar double release. I practiced it twice as much as any other skill. Ten times more than some. I worked on it and I worked on it, and then I worked on it some more. To be honest, I never really *liked* doing it because I frequently crashed. But I did it anyway. Always with the memory of a missed world title.

By the time the Olympics came around, that double release and I were a lot more comfortable. Not quite eight months after the fall in Budapest I jumped up and grabbed the bar in the all-around finals at the Olympic Games. About a minute later I came back down—when I was supposed to. I scored a perfect 10 on the high bar.

So looking back (it's always easier looking back) I can say I'm glad I failed in Budapest. Sometimes it's *necessary* to fail. That's how we learn. It wasn't fun when it happened, but it taught me how important it is to focus on what you need to focus on, not what you would like to focus on. Respecting a risk is every bit as important as taking one. Maybe more important.

If I hadn't fallen off that high bar in the world championships I might have continued to take that skill for granted, not trained it appropriately, then fallen off the high bar when the pressure was even greater, quite possibly not winning any Olympic medals at all. And right now you would instead be reading a book written by some ex-baseball player.

When I talk to corporate audiences about risk, I like to begin with that story about my fall in Budapest because it combines so many of the important elements of taking risks—and, OK, because it has a happy ending.

The point is, I needed that risk. I could have never realized my potential without it. But I also needed to respect it. We all need risks. The challenge is to know how to control them, instead of letting them control us.

The discussion about risks that follows explores ways in which sensible, calculated risk-taking can help us get where we want to go, instead of where the risks want to take us.

Is It Worth It?

The first questions we should ask ourselves is if a risk is worth it. What's the potential? Is it a risk that can help us make progress toward our goal?

Sometimes the "best" risks are those that require going against the grain, against what is popular, against what is cool. Some of these unpopular risks we'll decide simply aren't worth it. We'll determine that the potential negatives outweigh the potential positives. But some we'll decide are worth it.

Like the chance I took with gymnastics.

I took an unpopular social risk—and I knew it—when I made gymnastics my sport of choice. It's true that I've wound up getting a certain amount of acclaim from gymnastics. In the long run, the sport has been amazingly good to me. But when I was in junior high school and high school, being a gymnast was a risky move for me. I suspected it wasn't going to get me elected student body president or a date with the head cheerleader (right on both counts). I knew it wasn't going to make me popular. I knew by doing it I risked being ostracized by the others kids at school. It's important in junior high and high school to be "normal," and gymnastics was anything but normal.

But gymnastics fit me (all 5' 5-1/2" and 125 pounds of me) and I felt like I fit gymnastics. I suspected I had a shot at being decent at it (I was short, compact, and wasn't afraid of falling off things). Deep down I sensed it was a risk worth taking.

Sometimes I look back and wonder what if I had chosen football because everybody did football (I'd be dead!), or what if I had chosen some other sport just so I could belong? What if all that had mattered to me was doing what was popular? Look at what I'd have missed. I've had all these incredible experiences in my life that are tied into gymnastics. I'd have missed all of them if I hadn't decided that what I liked and what I was going to do was one of the most unpopular sports for male athletes in the United States of America.

Oh, I played the popular sports. Basketball, baseball. I played on my high school soccer team almost solely so I could feel like I was part of my school. It didn't interfere with my gymnastics workouts and Mako never even knew. I was center forward. We never won a game and I never scored a goal, but I played a lot and it made me feel better.

Mostly, though, I was an uncool gymnast. I know, that's easy to say now, but it was a reality when I was growing up. What I did was not mainstream, it was not popular, it did not make me "cool." I don't think anyone in my high school ever watched me compete in gymnastics. A lot of the faculty would come to my meets, but nobody my age came, and this was when I was a member of the U.S. national team. Everybody at school thought, *Gymnastics? What's that all about?* Before I'd get on the bus to go to the gym for a workout, my classmate would say, "So, you going to work out in your pajamas again today, Peter?" When it came to sweats, I was a few years ahead of the times. It seems funny now, because everybody travels in sweats.

I'm just thankful I had enough of an independent streak and self-confidence—and it was due primarily to the efforts of my family and my coaches—to go my own way. I felt free to chart my own course and not get bogged down by worrying how I measured up in the eyes of everyone else. We can spend a lot of time in life comparing ourselves with others. The problem is we're always going to find someone who is better or smarter or taller or nicer looking or richer or dresses better. The list is endless. I think it's dangerous—for kids especially—when life revolves around comparisons to others. It sets up conditions ripe for dangerous choices, disappointment and defeat. It's only when we compare ourselves to ourselves that we lay the foundation for contentment and success, and free ourselves up to take those calculated risks that might otherwise be looked at as too unpopular to consider.

Sorry, No Guarantees

Ever since I can remember, I've been interested in the Olympics. Long before I got active in gymnastics, and that was at age 11, I was already mesmerized by the Olympic Games. I watched the Games when they were on TV and read about them whenever I could. Olympic stories fascinated me as a boy and still do. Every four years, when TV, radio, or a corporation calls and asks if I'll work the Olympics, I can't believe my good fortune—I get to go to the Games in person, and get paid to do it!

One of my earliest personal Olympic memories dates back to 1972 when I was 10 years old. The Games were held in Munich that year and there was considerable anticipation about the expected showdown in the 1,500 meter run—the "metric mile"—between Kip Keino of Kenya and the American mile hero (now Congressman) Jim Ryun. Ryun was the world record-holder in both the mile and the 1,500. But in the 1968 Olympic Games held in Mexico City, it had been Keino, the Kenyan, who'd edged Ryun and won the gold medal. For four years, their Olympic rematch in Munich was eagerly awaited.

But the rematch never even happened. I was watching the opening heats of the 1,500 on television when Jim Ryun got caught between several runners during his qualifying heat and, in an effort to break loose, stumbled and fell to the track. It took him eight seconds to get to his feet, but by now he was nearly one hundred meters behind and it was impossible to make up the ground. He limped to the finish line with a bruised hip, a skinned knee, and maybe a sprained ankle. That fall wound up effectively sending Jim Ryun into retirement, and me into my bedroom in tears. I couldn't believe what had happened to my hero—and in the Olympics, of all places. I found myself wishing I could go to the Olympics, and avenge Jim Ryun's fall.

While that experience made for a disappointing day for a 10-year-old (not to mention for Jim Ryun), his dramatic "fall" does, these many years later, provide us with an object lesson in risk-taking—one that we'd all do well to remember. No matter who we are or what we've accomplished—and no matter how well we've prepared—there are always going to be risks if we decide to enter the race. And sometimes, the risks are going to win.

There are no guarantees, in other words. That's an important concept to understand when it comes to risks. It's important to remember that danger, in its many forms, is an inherent part of risk-taking. No matter how calculating and careful we may be, there's always going to be the chance for some kind of harm, whether it's physical, mental, or emotional.

Pure Inspiration

The best example I've ever personally seen of a person accepting risk and dealing with difficult consequences involved Mark Caso.

If you could go back to 1979 and see Peter Vidmar and Mark Caso working out in Los Angeles you'd see two guys imitating the workout scenes from the *Rocky* movies. We were roommates and we'd wake up every morning at 5:45 to run up Janns Steps at the center of the UCLA campus. Then we'd go to the gym and work out, and then we'd work out some more. We were both obsessed and probably a little nuts. We were both on a mission to make the United States gymnastics team for the 1980 Olympic Games in Moscow.

Mark was from New York, where he was coached into one of the top high school gymnasts in the country by his father, Ron, at a gymnastics club called Dynamo in Syracuse. We met during our senior years of high school when we roomed together at the McDonald's National High School All-Around Invitational. I'd already signed to attend UCLA but Mark hadn't yet decided where he was going to go to college. I said he ought to come to UCLA and talked him into visiting the campus. He flew to L.A. a few weeks later, in early April. Back in Syracuse it was still something like fifty below after you factored in the wind chill factor. He got off the plane and said "What are these?" I raised my left eyebrow and said, "Palm trees." He said, "Wow, can I touch one?" "Whatever." Within an hour he called home. "Mom," I heard him say, "I'm coming here." He hadn't even seen the campus yet! That's what passes for strategic college sports recruiting at UCLA: At the end of winter, bring in the recruits from the East.

Mark was an outstanding all-around gymnast. He was particularly good at floor exercise. There was no better tumbler on the team. He had a skill in his routine called a one and a half twisting one and three quarter dive roll. He'd do it on his third pass down the mat and it called for a rollout instead of landing on your feet. It was a difficult skill, a good one for the risk points, and Mark had the talent to do it. But one day during practice midway into our freshman year, when he came out of that risky skill he landed short, crunched on the back of his head . . . and broke his neck.

Practice came to a standstill as Mark lay there temporarily paralyzed. An ambulance and paramedics crew arrived and he was rushed to the hospital where he slowly started to get his movement back. Emphasis on slowly. They fit him with a halo brace by drilling four holes into his skull and they placed his entire body in traction. He was surrounded by sandbag weights attached to pulleys. He hadn't broken any bones but he'd basically compressed the vertebrae and torn all the supporting ligaments. They had to put him in traction and attach the sandbag weights to try to straighten everything back out.

After a few days of that they operated, taking a bone from his hip and fusing it to the fifth and sixth cervical vertebrae.

Several weeks and two more braces later, he was finally out of the hospital. As soon as he was able, he came back to the gym, if only to sit on the sidelines and stretch a little. In a few short weeks he'd gone from being a person who could do practically anything he wanted with his body to a point where he couldn't even move his fingers—and now he was finally back in the gym starting anew, like a five-year-old, learning forward and backward rolls and handstands all over again.

Needless to say, seeing Mark back at square one had a sobering effect on the rest of us, his teammates. Just as seeing his comeback had an inspirational effect.

Whereas many would have checked out of gymnastics forever after such an accident—and no one would have questioned why—

Mark checked back in with the same relentlessness that had once gotten him out of bed at 5:45 and climbing those campus stairs. If anything, now he was even more driven. He started from scratch and he didn't stop. His energy had an enormous positive effect on the rest of us in the gym. When you've got a guy next to you who can't even do remedial gymnastics but he's working as hard as ever, it makes it a lot tougher to complain about your own sore ankles or the torn blisters in your hand.

Mark's attitude was that he knew the inherent risks of gymnastics going in and he wasn't going to feel sorry for himself because one of those risks had made him pay a price. There was no way he was going to quit.

The result was a comeback almost too amazing to be believed. In the 1981 United States championships, just fifteen months after he broke his neck, Mark Caso placed seventh in the all-around. You can look it up.

Although he came close, he never did make an Olympic team, but in his own way he went far beyond that. He now runs a successful business in Los Angeles.

Second Chances

If we're lucky, we get at least a second chance to give a risk its "proper respect." Such was the case for me after my "fall" at the world championships in Budapest. At the 1996 Olympic Games in Atlanta, the gold-medal winning decathlete, Dan O'Brien, served as yet another example of getting it right . . . the second time.

O'Brien had been the favorite to win the decathlon gold medal four years before Atlanta, in Barcelona. But he never even made it to the Barcelona Games. At the U.S. Track & Field Trials O'Brien nonchalantly passed several early-round heights in the pole vault, confident he could clear the bar as it went higher up the standards. But he wound up putting too much pressure on himself as a result. He wound up missing all three of his pole vault tries and the resulting no-height cost him the top three finish he needed to qualify for the Olympics. Despite the fact he was the defending world decathlon champion, and already listed as the odds-on favorite to win in Barcelona, he wasn't even able to make the trip.

In qualifying for Atlanta, O'Brien took care to jump as early as possible in the pole vault. He was taking no chances this time around.

Calculated—and Uncalculated—Risks

A calculated risk is clearly in focus, well understood, and after careful consideration is seen as worth taking. The risks we've already talked about all fit into the "calculated" category. Mark Caso was dealing with calculated risks, so was Jim Ryun, and so was I in junior high school when I decided to be an "unpopular" gymnast.

An uncalculated risk, on the other hand, is neither researched or understood. It's not something we're prepared for. Usually, it's just plain stupid.

We're susceptible to these uncalculated risks when we let our guard down long enough to not consider whether the potential consequences are worth the gamble.

As an example of "stupid" risk-taking, I'll use myself.

When it comes to recreational pursuits, I tend more toward the adventurous more than the cerebral. When I stopped competing in gymnastics I did not "retire" into more laid-back, sedentary sports such as golf.

Instead of moving into golf, or tennis, after leaving competitive gymnastics, I moved straight into—mountain biking, believe it or not. I found that mountain biking provided a natural segue out of gymnastics. I immediately found that I loved just everything about the sport—the training involved, the demands on the body, the thrill of walking into a bike shop and buying the latest accessory (or the latest bike). I love the adrenalin rush you can get on a steep, tricky descent. In some ways it's like gymnastics but without the judges.

And to be honest I'd have to say I love the risks. So far, I have thirteen stitches, two sprained wrists, torn ankle ligaments, and a separated shoulder to show for it. What a sport!

But, whereas when I started out in gymnastics, I was always being made constantly aware of the importance of only taking risks when it was necessary and prudent; in mountain biking that wasn't the case. For one thing, I wasn't training to try to be the best in the world, making sure I systematically touched every step along the way. And for another thing, remember, I had a coach in gymnastics. Even when I wanted to do something stupid, Mr. Mako wouldn't let me.

But in mountain biking, all I had was me. When I took it up, I just climbed on the saddle and started riding.

My competitive instincts kicked in quickly and I decided I wanted to race.

I entered my first race in the early spring in the hills near Camp Pendleton, California, a Marine base not far from my home. I'd hired a former Olympic cyclist named David Brinton to set me up on a rigid schedule. I'd trained all through the fall and winter. I'd ridden on the trails behind my house when I was in town and, when I was on the road speaking, I would make it a point to find somewhere that I could work out on a stationary bike. My obsessiveness got me to the point where I could beat everybody in my neighborhood except my neighbor and friend, Todd Brown, a veteran cyclist and competitive racer.

Together, Todd and I went to Camp Pendleton. I elected to bypass the Beginner category and entered the Sport category, just one level in back of the Experts. I'd been training hard for eight months. I figured I was ready. Then the race began and I immediately realized one thing: I wasn't going to win this race. On the very first ascent, a really steep rise, a lead group sprinted ahead and Todd went with them. I didn't. I just couldn't. Over many years and countless miles, those guys had developed the lungs, the legs, and the know-how to deal with these conditions, and despite my short-term intensive training, I wasn't there. Well, most of them were in that kind of shape. I did take some satisfaction in passing guys who went out too fast and were now on the side of the road assuming the hurl position.

But, still, I was determined to finish as high as I could and when the racecourse switched from uphill to downhill—a steep, rutted, gnarly section called Iron Mike—I soon realized that I was going downhill fast. Going downhill was my forte—who'd have thought? I was lighter than most of the racers, and that should have been to my disadvantage on the downhill, but probably as a result of my gymnastics training I had pretty good balance on the descent. So I just let 'er fly. And to me, hey, the faster the better.

On the second lap I again lost ground going uphill, but made it up, and more, on the descent. I was beginning to like this. Good old Iron Mike was my ticket to a better finish.

Then came the third lap. Again, I experienced some serious lung loss on the climb. Again, I got to the descent and started to fly . . .

. . . and fly

. . . and fly . . .

I didn't even see the rut. I didn't even have time to brake. I probably sailed ten feet through the air before I came back to earth, still holding onto my handlebars. Well, half of my handlebars. They had snapped when my front wheel hit square into the rut, catapulting me forward like I'd been shot out of a cannon. I landed on roots and dirt and weeds and rolled another thirty or forty feet, tearing the skin off my back. "Don't move!" someone yelled as a guy carrying a medicine kit ran toward me, and I thought, "I'm not going to move!" because by now I was mad. In the space of less than an hour I'd gone from *"Isn't this a great sport"* to *"I can't wait till this is over"* to *"You are an idiot!"*

I had three speeches to give later that same week, each one involving a pommel horse demonstration—and I couldn't move my shoulder, my wrists felt like they'd just tried to lift a locomotive, and my ribs didn't feel so hot either.

At that I was lucky. I went to the doctor and the official diagnosis was a "grade two" separation of the shoulder, sore wrists and bruised ribs. Nothing life-threatening, and nothing, as it turned out, other than pain to stop me. I taped my wrists heavily, wore wrist braces, took as much ibuprofen as possible, iced the whole way out on the flight, covered up the scars as best I could, and, forty-eight hours after the crash, somehow got through my corporate speech and pommel horse routine.

I could have called in sick and cancelled the speech, but I didn't think it was right that a group that had scheduled my appearance and was counting on my being there should have to pay for my stupidity.

I'd taken some uncalculated risks—and I was paying the price.

There are some limits to risk-taking that I think should always be in place. When you push the envelope too much it's called foolishness. I never got to that point in gymnastics, but I did in my first mountain bike race.

Preparation—There's Nothing Like It

That mountain bike experience is hardly the only time I learned the hard way about the importance of having the right equipment and enough experience before tackling a risk. You want more example of being stupid? I've got plenty.

Besides gymnastics, I grew up enamored of surfing. Believe it or not, I was a beach boy. I was born and raised near the famous southern California surf, listening to the Beach Boys and "Surfin' USA" and watchin' dudes drivin' woodies. My oldest brother, John, surfed at the same famous surf spots with Dewey Webber and others who were the greats of the '60's when surfing was coming into its own. He still surfs. I remember how he used to laugh at the beach blanket bingo image because he knew that wasn't real surfing.

Anyway, I grew up in that atmosphere and when I was 14 I began surfing myself. By then I was heavily into gymnastics but I liked surfing too much to quit. The summer when I was 14 turned out to be my own personal Endless Summer, one that just seemed to last forever. Every morning my friend Sam Tipp, who was also on the gymnastics team, and I would take the bus from Ladera Heights to El Porto Beach, near El Segundo and Manhattan Beach. We'd surf all day long, and I mean all day, and then catch the last bus back home so we could get cleaned up and make it to gymnastics practice. Mako was working at a bank during the days and so the practices were all at night, which worked out great for my dual life.

The problem, of course, was that surfing isn't exactly a sedentary sport. You paddle all day, you ride the waves, others ride you. I'd come home exhausted, waterlogged and sunbaked (and, of course, as we liked to say back then, "stoked")—and then go to the gym, where my biggest fear was this: What if Mako found out?! Worse yet, What if Mako found out and told me to stop surfing?!

The problem was, if Mako ever said, "Hey Pete, I know you're surfing and I want you to cut it out," I would have stopped. No question. He was the boss. My only solution was to keep my surfing a complete secret from him.

I knew the best thing for me to do was never let on that I was tired. So I tried to be extraordinarily perky at practice, always ready to go, constantly excited. My hair was bleached white and I was dark brown I was so suntanned but Sam and I never mentioned one word about surfing that entire summer—and, amazingly, Mako never asked.

The demands of gymnastics and, later on, college studies at UCLA, conspired to gradually bring my surfing to a virtual halt.

But it was always in my brain, and not long after the Olympics—and my "retirement" from gymnastics—I found myself back in the waves. I was on assignment for ESPN, commentating on a gymnastics competition between China and the United States in Honolulu.

I was there for a week and ESPN's budget wouldn't allow me to bring my wife. So I brought the next best thing, my surfboard. We had a lot of catching up to do.

All was fine until I had a free day and Bart Conner, who was watching the meet with his coach/manager Paul Ziert, and I decided to rent a Jeep and drive around the island of Oahu. I brought along my board.

This was in February and when we got to the north side of the island I got a look for the first time at the legendary north shore surf breaks. I'd read about these waves in Surfing magazine since I was a kid. I recognized the breaks and the beaches just from the photos I'd seen and the descriptions I'd read.

When we got to what I knew was the Vatican of surfing, I asked Bart to stop the Jeep.

"Gotta be Sunset Beach," I said.

"Gotta go out there."

So I grabbed my board and paddled out into some of the world's biggest and most legendary surf. Which was fine except for I was paddling out on my 6-foot-4 tri-fin board, the kind of small-sized surfboard that just shreds the waves at Manhattan Beach, but at Sunset looks like a toothpick in a bathtub. There probably wasn't another board out there under eight and a half feet—big wave guns. Anybody with half a brain knows when the waves break at ten to fifteen feet you don't go out on a 6-4 board, and especially if you're not a great surfer who hasn't been surfing for the past eight years.

The problem was, this realization dawned on me only after I'd already paddled out into the jaws of Sunset.

To my credit, I like to think, I began to reconsider once I saw the waves up close and personal. The drops were the size of houses. Big houses.

Every time a wave came through, I'd decline to take off. The faces were huge; they must have been twenty feet. I kept drifting back toward shore, thinking I'd ride a smaller wave back to the beach. But as I was having difficulty finding a wave small enough, sure enough, as every surfer knows, it came time for a set to come through. A set is a series of big waves, usually three or four, that comes through every ten or twelve minutes or so.

It was at this point that I turned around to size up my situation, and I saw The Poseiden Adventure!, a.k.a. the first wave in the set, out there on the horizon, coming toward me. I had two choices: I could either paddle straight toward the big wave and hope to make it over the face before it broke, or I could turn around and paddle in the direction of the shore, hoping to outrun the break and maybe ride the whitewater to shore.

I chose to paddle into the wave. I paddled and paddled and paddled. About the time I was approaching complete blowout shoulder fatigue I looked up and realized . . . wrong choice!

I wasn't going to make it. If I kept going it would be like running headlong into a brick wall, so in the spirit of damage control I stopped the only momentum I could stop—mine—and braced myself for the collision. I took my board, threw it as far to the side as my seven-foot leash, which tethered me by my ankle to the board, would allow, and took in as much breath as possible. Then I felt this whoosh! and the wave hit me and my first thought was, that wasn't so bad, but then the Maytag cycle began and I got sucked in and so did my board and now I've got another worry— what if the board, which is pointed at the top and no longer in my control, whacks me?

So I'm in the spin cycle, covering my head with my arms, waiting for the board to hit me. I soon forgot about that because

I realized I was running out of air. That's when I got to that horrible point where you stop thinking about surfing, about bodily injury, and start thinking about your wife and children—and realize you've actually done something stupid enough it could end your life.

Then, finally, I hit foam! No air, just foam. The foam is about five feet thick in waves that big. But it gave me new hope and I fought through the foam and finally, just when I was sure I was going to black out, I broke through. I gulped in oxygen, filling my lungs, just in time to turn around and see . . . another wave. Whammmmm! Right on top of me. I go through the spin cycle again. I fight through the foam. Luckily it's a smaller wave. When I emerged from that one I staggered back onto my board. I looked at a guy from New Jersey I'd met about ten minutes earlier. He also looked like he'd just spent time in a blender. He said, "What did you think of that?" I said, "I'm going in."

Bart and Paul hadn't even been watching. They said, "Hey Pete, how'd it go? How was it?" I said fine. My competitive side wouldn't let me tell them I'd just had a near-death experience.

I learned a lesson about risk-taking that day. There's no percentage in taking risks when you're ill-equipped to deal with them; when you haven't thought them through. I should have had a bigger board, and I should have spent a few more months getting into surfing shape before I ever even paddled out at Sunset.

Every day we face risks in all the facets of our lives. Some may be physical, some may be mental. In business, in relationships, in driving our cars, you name it. If we play the stock market, that's a risk. If we cross the street. If we ride a roller coaster. The list is endless. Most worthwhile pursuits involve risk. But no matter what form risk-taking takes, the basic formula for success is the same. As much as possible, risks should be taken only with eyes wide open, with consequences clearly understood, and when we're armed with all the knowledge, experience, and equipment that's available.

Timing Is Everything

Some risks are worth taking under certain circumstances, and not under others. Risks should be taken when it's going to matter, but when it isn't going to matter, steer clear.

Timing, in other words, is just about everything.

Using gymnastics as a case in point, that means going for it all out in a competition, but not necessarily in the gym. There are times when it's much wiser and more productive to exercise patience and make sure a risky skill is put together methodically and with care.

And anything with long odds attached to it, you save until there's no reason NOT to use it.

As an alum, I'm a big UCLA fan. In the spring of '95, when the UCLA basketball team was playing in the NCAA basketball tournament, I was in front of the TV, watching every game. I tend to be an optimist but I have to admit, in the second round of the tournament, when Missouri went ahead of the Bruins by a point with 4.8 seconds to play in the game, I was not encouraged. UCLA called time out to sort out the fix it was in.

The inbounds pass came to Tyus Edney, a senior guard and, at 5' 10", the shortest player on the floor. As soon as the ball touched Edney's hands the clock started, and so did he. He dribbled through the Missouri until he got to the other end of the floor, where he pivoted around one defender at the top of the key, cut into the lane, and just before time ran out, hooked a layup over a player almost a foot taller.

The ball went through the bottom of the net just as the buzzer sounded to end the game. UCLA won by one. Eight days and three games later, the Bruins were the national collegiate basketball champions.

What I later learned about that final play is that to Tyus Edney it wasn't as risky as it looked to all of us who watched it. At the end of UCLA's practices all year long he had worked on that play. The Bruins hoped they'd never be in a position where they had to use that play. There wasn't a lot of room for error. But if a game ever called for it, they had that play. Just in case.

Until the second round of the championship tournament—in the Bruins' twenty-ninth game of the year—there had been no circumstances that had called for the Tyus Edney play.

But now it was either that play or go home early and Edney was ready. He knew 4.8 seconds was enough time for him to make it to the basket because he'd done it hundreds of times in practice in less time than that. As he stood on the court awaiting the inbounds pass he wasn't weighed down with doubt about not having enough time, or with what he'd do when he got to the other end. What he was about to do was risky, sure, but if he did it the way he'd practiced, it *could* work. It *was* possible.

So he went to work and turned himself into a hero.

If You've Got It . . . Flaunt It

There is probably no greater example of risk takers at the Olympics than aerial freestyle skiers. And the 2002 games in Salt Lake City didn't disappoint us. In aerials, a competitor chooses what jump he's going to do based on variables such as strength of field, weather conditions (especially wind) and how his fellow competitors have done. Each competitor does two jumps in the finals. Everybody does their first jump and then goes in order of first-jump finish for the second jump. There are five judges for air and form and two judges for landing. Highest score is a 7.0. In the Olympics, twelve guys were in the finals at the aerials hill at Deer Valley.

For their first jump, almost all of them did quad-twisting combinations—triple somersaults with four twists in the air—

that had a degree of difficulty of 4.450 (5.0 is the highest, which is considered near impossible, and 4.450 is pretty much the difficulty ceiling). At the end of the first jump, Ales Valenta of the Czech Republic found himself tied for fifth place, square in the middle of the field and out of the medals. Eric Bergoust of the United States led after a near-perfect score of 130.38 for his first jump, followed by Alexei Grichin of Belarus at 129.49, Joe Pack of the United States at 129.49, Jeff Bean of Canada at 128.60 and then Dmitri Dashinski and Valenta at 127.04. By way of background, Berqoust was the defending Olympic champion from Nagano and the heavy favorite, with Grichin the next favored jumper, and Pack, a Park City resident, the heavy local favorite. In other words, not only was Valenta two spots away from medaling, he was trailing a very strong field. Jumping seventh in the final round, with Bean, Pack, Grichin and Bergoust still to jump, Valenta needed something more than just a good, solid jump. He needed spectacular.

Which is why he decided it was high time to unsheath his secret weapon—namely, a back double full, double full, full. In English, that's a triple back flip with *five* twists. In aerials history, a five-twist jump had only been landed on snow four times—all by Valenta—and only once had it been landed in competition—by Valenta in a World Cup earlier in the winter. Needless to say, it's a risky jump. An aerialist has six seconds, maximum, to do everything he's going to do in the air. Three somersaults with five twists is pushing it. The degree of difficulty rating for Valenta's jump is 4.850, almost the limit. But Valenta needed just such a jump if he wanted to have a serious shot at winning. In Nagano he'd finished fourth, one step from the podium. For four years he'd plotted and planned to have a different result this time. At the top of the in-run before his second jump, he looked at the windsock atop the officials tower. It was barely fluttering. The day was slightly overcast. The snow was hard. Conditions were close to perfect. Valenta had already filed his choice of jump with the judges—a "bdfdff" in aerials shorthand—and if he was going to change his choice, he'd have to do so in the next few seconds. Instead, he turned his skis downhill and was off.

Six seconds later, he came back to earth with a landing that was slightly off-balance but solid—and he had become the first man in Olympic aerials history to successfully perform a five-twist flip. He scored a 129.98, giving him a 257.02 two-jump total. His name went to the top of the leaderboard. The next four competitors, each selecting a jump with a 4.450 degree of difficulty, all had a chance to overtake Valenta with solid effort. But Valenta's breakthrough leap seemed to, if not unnerve them, at least subdue them. Canada's Bean scored 122.37 and Belarus's Grichin scored 121.48. Then came Park City's own Joe Pack, who scored 122.15 for a 251.64 total—almost six full points behind Valenta. Now only Berqoust, the 32-year-old king of aerials, was left to jump. After his opening total of 130.38 Berqoust could knock Valenta out of first place with a solid score of 127 or higher. He wouldn't have to be great, just very good. But in his exuberance, Bergoust got too much air on his takeoff and couldn't handle the landing. His crash cost him dearly, relegating him to a final-jump score of 88.11 and a last-place finish. Bergoust admitted that the pressure Valenta had put on made him jump a little beyond himself, spelling his doom. As for Valenta, who had suffered a broken collarbone just two weeks earlier and had a titanium plate inserted in his shoulder, he said there was no question in his mind that he had to risk everything and go for the quintuple flip, even if no one had ever landed such a jump in the Olympics. "The weather was good. Not much wind," he said. "I'd practiced it all summer. I knew I could do it."

For a Good Time . . .

When risks become allies, not adversaries—that's when the fun begins.

Those individuals who truly embrace risk-taking stand out from the crowd. In American business annals, few examples illustrate what I'm talking about better than former Chrysler Corporation chairman Lee Iacocca.

In 1979, when he took over as chairman of Chrysler Corporation, neither Iacocca nor Chrysler was in good shape. Iacocca was 55 years old and recently fired from Ford Motor Co., where he'd worked more than half his life. Chrysler, still holding on to its traditional line of gas-guzzling cars despite an Iranian revolution that had driven up gasoline prices, was skidding toward what looked like certain bankruptcy. When Iacocca tried to borrow money in an effort to turn things around, more than one hundred of the country's biggest banks turned him down.

But Lee Iacocca was prepared to take risks. He showed that he was willing to risk both personal and corporate embarassment of truly monumental proportions when he then went to the federal government and asked for a loan of $1.5 billion.

He gave Congress the sales pitch that if Chrysler went out of business it would cost U.S. taxpayers nearly $3 billion in unemployment compensation, to say nothing of further crippling the economy. But, he contended, $1.5 billion in federally backed loan guarantees wouldn't cost taxpayers anything, he said, because Chrysler would pay the money back—and they had Lee Iacocca's word on it.

With that brash pledge, Iacocca succeeded in getting the federal government loan guarantees. With them, he was able to turn Chrysler from a dying company into one of the biggest success stories in American business history. A new line of products that featured the LeBaron convertible and the Chrysler/Plymouth minivans was introduced. For the good of the cause, Chrysler's union workers agreed to temporary pay cuts and plant and job cutbacks. Iacocca himself appealed to the American public via television ads to give Chrysler another chance to prove that "Made in America" still meant something. And to show that he was willing to personally sacrifice, he gave himself a salary of just one dollar a year, along with stock options that wouldn't be worth anything unless the company got back to full fiscal health.

The result was unprecedented growth. Everything worked. Every penny of the federally backed loans was paid back by 1983, seven years ahead of the final due date. Chrysler was back in the black—and all because of a man who was willing to take a risk.

Enjoy

Risk-taking is the difference between spectating and participating. As Theodore Roosevelt, the twenty-sixth president of the United States, once said:

> "It is not the critic who counts, not the man who points out how the strong man stumbled, or where the doer of deeds could have done them better, the credit belongs to the man who is actually in the arena, whose face is marred by dust and sweat and blood; who strives valiantly; who errs and comes short again and again; who knows the great enthusiasms, the great devotions, and spends himself in a worthy cause; who, at the best, knows in the end the triumph of high achievement; and who, at the worst, if he fails, at least fails while daring greatly, so that his place shall never be with those cold and timid souls who know neither victory nor defeat."

Risk-taking is what Roosevelt is talking about. It has its own built-in reward system. He discovered that personally as a sickly child who refused to rest and coddle himself as his family's doctors suggested. Instead, he threw himself into rigorous exercise and public service. As a result he became a rugged outdoorsman who enjoyed excellent health—and became the president of his country.

It's the journey, risks and all, that matters.

Once on a speaking assignment I found myself at Andrews Air Force Base in San Antonio, Texas, where I was addressing a group of Air Force recruiters. I was excited, because all my life I'd fantasized about being a jet pilot, and here I was in the midst of jet pilots, talking about risk, originality and virtuosity. I happened to mention to the commanders my fascination with jets. I told them I lived near the El Toro Marine base in California, I had friends who were fighter pilots, and ever since I could remember I'd been interested in jets. I'd always wondered if I'd missed my calling. Maybe I should have been a pilot. What was it like, I wondered, to do gymnastics in the sky.

After I dropped enough hints, they asked me if I'd like to go on an orientation flight in a T-38. A T-38 is the jet the Air Force uses to train its pilots. If you ever saw the movie *Top Gun*, the planes that were painted black to represent Soviet MIGs, were F-5s, which are a combat version of the T-38.

Of course, I jumped at the chance to fly in a T-38, and after I'd gone through what they call egress procedure—where I was given the basic orientation about the airplane and about ejection procedures—I found myself wearing an authentic G-suit, ready to fly. A G-suit has a bladder that molds around your legs and injects air into the bladder commensurate to the number of Gs you're pulling. One G is equal to the acceleration of gravity. Whenever you accelerate faster than gravity, the body has definite reactions to it, none of them particularly comfortable. A G-suit helps counterbalance those effects. The more Gs you pull, the more your suit squeezes, causing your blood to continue flowing upward. Otherwise, you're susceptible to what they call G-LOC, which stands for Gravity Induced Loss of Consciousness.

They also instruct you to tense every muscle in your body and grunt—another self-defense tactic against G-LOC.

I had two goals: Don't pass out, and don't throw up.

I wound up going one for two.

It was a tremendous experience, more exhilerating than I'd even imagined. We took off side by side with another T-38 and the first thing the pilot said was "OK, we're going to test your G-suit." All of a sudden, vroooooooom, just like that, we banked to the left. We pulled four Gs. I looked for the plane that had been right next to us and it was a mile away.

I was feeling fine at this point, when the pilot said, "Do you want to do a loop? We'll pull a lot of Gs on this one."

I said let's go for it, and he pulled on the stick and as we went upside down the G meter shot up to six, which made me the equivalent of a 780-pound man. I kept thinking, "Don't pass out," grunting and tensing all my muscles. Then we were upright again.

We continued to do dips and rolls and loops as we maneuevered with the other plane. We did some other maneuvers, banking from side to side, pulling four and five G's just nonstop. The pilots were having a great time. These are people who really enjoy their work.

Everything was great until I took the stick. I made the mistake of telling the pilot that I had flown an F-18 stimulator at El Toro. A simulator! I had simulated an aerlieron roll where they spin the plane 360 degrees. He said "Pete, do you want to try an aerlieron roll? Go for it!" So I gave it a try. I did it very slowly the first time. He said I should do it faster. I did. Much faster. The plane spun around quickly, almost violently. So did my stomach. "Tom," I said to the pilot. "I'm feeling a bit queasy." (A subtle way of saying, "Dude, I'm gonna hurl!").

As we were flying over downtown San Antonio I got to see what I'd had for lunch—again. I remember picking up my bag and waving it to the guys in the other plane like some kind of trophy. Later they told me they had a name for what I'd done. "Lunch time," they call it.

After the flight I talked with the pilots about their flying and the risks involved with it. The ultimate potential risk, of course, would be in the event of war, where experiencing "lunch time" is the least of your worries.

It was impossible to come away from that experience with those fighter pilots without sensing their enthusiasm for life. It's an enthusiasm I've found permeates from those who, as Roosevelt said, don't just sit idly by, but are in the arena, getting dirty and participating in the fight. Risk-takers, in other words.

Looked at in this context, risk-taking goes beyond just a necessary step, beyond just a requirement to reach the perfect 10. Risks—sensible, calculated, prudent, rational risks—are the obstacles that make reaching the destination worth it. Without them there would be no struggle, and no satisfaction.

Triumphs that are truly meaningful are triumphs that require effort. If there wasn't rough on the golf course, could you appreciate it as much when you drive a golf ball dead in the middle of the fairway? If the marlin just jumped in your boat, would catching them be as satisfying? If not for risks, rewards would lose much of their value. They just wouldn't be worth as much

Risks give life its zip. Approached sensibly, they bring excitement, they bring exhilaration, they bring zest, they bring fun, they bring inspiration, and they bring satisfaction and results. Risks are what make things that otherwise might seem impossible suddenly come into view as *possible*. No one is exempt from this formula. As long as we're willing to learn from where we've been, and willing to get back up when we fall, risk-taking is a plus. A big plus. In my opinion, the world could use a lot more of it. Once again, instead of asking "Why?" we should often times ask "Why not?"

Remember *Rocky*? There is a scene in the movie that to me epitomizes the kind of attitude we all should have when it comes to stretching beyond ourselves and taking calculated risks.

Rocky's girl friend, Adrian, has been listening to her brother, Paulie, run down Rocky's chances, until finally she's had enough.

"Well," she tells him, "Roosevelt finished last in his class.

"And Beethoven was deaf,

"And Helen Keller was blind . . .

". . . I think Rocky has a good chance."

Originality

" ... Two roads diverged in a wood and I, I took the one
less traveled by, and that has made all the difference."

ROBERT FROST

"What if we was to push the outside of the envelope?"

CHUCK YEAGER IN THE RIGHT STUFF

WHEN I WAS 13 I used to read my copy of *International Gymnast* just
before I'd go to bed. Then I'd turn out the lights and lie there
and try to imagine the best gymnastics routine there ever was or
ever could be. The ultimate performance.

They'd print the routines of the world's great gymnasts in *International Gymnast* and I'd memorize them all. They were my guide. They'd do a skill-by-skill of, say, Mitsuo Tsukahara, the great gymnast from Japan, from his latest meet. They'd list it all: Inverted giant, full on to vault catch . . . finish with half-in, half-out dismount . . . and so on and so on. My non-gymnastics friends would read these gymnastics "box scores" and ask if anybody ever did a double martini with a lemon twist.

But I knew what all these moves were and after I'd read about them I'd program them into my brain and then I'd call them up as I'd lie there, dreaming about the ultimate routine. I'd take this skill from Tsukahara, and another skill from the great Sawao Kato, and another from the Russian champion, Nikolai Andrianov. I'd put them all together in one super colossal routine in my mind and try to imagine doing that routine myself—and I'd laugh. "That's not going to happen," I'd think to myself. "Not to me. *That's* the ultimate."

Now fast forward ten years later, to the 1984 Olympic Games in Los Angeles. Every routine I performed there, and virtually every routine performed by every other gymnast in the competition, was light years beyond that "ultimate routine" I'd envisioned as an 11-year-old. A decade later, The Best Routine Ever was obsolete.

Over the years, I came to realize that it wasn't nearly as difficult imagining imitating what the best in the world *were doing* as it was imagining doing what they *weren't doing*.

I'm convinced it was that realization by my teammates and me that had more to do with our success in the 1984 Olympics than anything else. People ask what was special about that team, and I'd have to say that one factor was our ability to be innovative. Over a number of years, both individually and collectively, we'd managed to evolve from copycats into inventors, and that seemed to make all the difference.

Not that it was by any means an easy process. We had a pattern that was hard to break. We'd go to big events such as a World Championship. We'd walk into the gym for the training sessions, look across the gym and see a great gymnast from Russia or China or Japan jump up on the rings or the parallel bars and do something we'd never seen before, and our jaws would drop and we'd say "Wow!" "What a great trick!" "Why didn't we think of that?!"

Then we'd run back to the gym the next week and we'd learn it ourselves. Sometimes we'd find it wasn't even that hard to learn. It was just new.

By the next competition we'd show up, feeling impressed with ourselves because of what we'd learned, and walk in the gym, look across the floor, see the same guys working out we'd seen before, and watch them doing something totally new and innovative. Again, something we'd never seen before.

We'd say "Wow!" "What a great trick!" "Why didn't we think of that?"

And on and on the pattern would continue. Those other teams would get the originality points and we'd get nothing. We were just being copycats. We were always playing catchup—doing what they'd done last year.

But finally we came to our senses and realized we had to stop playing follow the leader. If we wanted to be successful, we had to get original ourselves. Once we realized that, that's when we put ourselves in a position to be contenders instead of just followers.

Originality is the most exciting part of my sport. Ask any gymnast. To be in a gym, to be working on something that maybe, just maybe, no one else has ever done before. That's exciting. (Well, at least until you stop and ask yourself this question: "Why is no one else trying this?" And then you think maybe they have, they just didn't survive).

Probably the best example of our "becoming original" prior to the 1984 Olympics was the Gaylord Flip, named after its inventor, Mitch Gaylord.

Describing the Gaylord Flip does not do it justice. You really have to see it to appreciate it. It is not for the faint of heart. It's a high bar skill that calls for letting go of the bar after a series of backward giant swings, doing a one and a half somersault with a half turn from the pike position over the bar, and finally catching the bar on the opposite side on your way back down. At the apex of the Gaylord Flip you're about fourteen feet above the ground, a good five feet above the bar, which is already nine feet off the floor.

When you're coming down, if you reach for the bar and the bar's not there . . . it can be a really ugly experience. (For reasons that should seem obvious, I have never tried it).

But if you catch the bar it can be an exhilarating, awe-inspiring experience. Which is how it turned out in the Olympics. Mitch did his flip—successfully—in two separate rounds and both times the judges not only gave him high marks for originality, but also for risk and virtuosity—all because of this one single original skill. When it comes to effective inventions, the Gaylord Flip definitely goes to the head of the originality class.

More amazing to me is the fact that almost two decades later hardly any gymnasts have even tried the Gaylord Flip in competition. That's how hard it is. That's astounding in a sport that I believe is the fastest moving sport in the world.

Of course Mitch took a long time to develop that skill. He didn't just walk in the gym one day and say "Hey, I've got a great idea guys, watch this," and then, after he'd done it flawlessly, announce that he was going to name it after himself.

It didn't work like that. It took a lot of time, practice, and experimenting. Most originality is like that. It begins with, "Hmmm, I've got a great idea, I wonder if it's possible." And then the work begins.

That's how it was with Mitch and his flip. He didn't even begin without first taking every precaution available. At first, he started with a spotting belt. This is a padded belt connected by ropes attached to pulleys in the ceiling of the gym. A spotting belt is what makes it possible to fall and not run into damaging objects, such as the bar or the floor. Someone, usually your coach, stands on the floor at the end of the rope and is supposed to pull on it before your face slams into the bar. (Hopefully the coach weighs more than you do). That's the idea.

But even that's not easy. In Mitch's case, he needed a tremendous amount of centrifugal force to do his skill successfully. He had to really be flying around the bar before he went into his somersault. In order to get enough momentum he had to do some giant swings first. But the problem is that he's got a rope attached to the spotting belt, connected to the ceiling which means before he can do the swings he first must wrap the rope around the bar in the opposite direction of the giant swings equal to the number of swings he's going to do before he lets go of the bar. Let go one swing too early, or one swing too late . . . and you have a human yo-yo.

Sometimes practice would come to a standstill when Mitch was in the exciting, early learning stages of the Gaylord Flip.

Sooner or later, spotting belts give way to the next line of defense—the foam pit. This is a pit sunk eight feet deep in the floor directly below the high bar. It's filled with about thirty thousand cubes of foam rubber and allows you to land on your face and still come up smiling, or at least with all your teeth. The first time Mitch did the skill without the spotting belts, he did it over a foam pit.

Finally, the moment of truth arrives. That's when it's just you, the high bar, the hard mat below, and a coach standing on that mat who may or may not catch you if you fall.

It wasn't until about eight months after he first conceived of the Gaylord Flip that Mitch finally tried it solo. It took time to become an original. With patience, with diligence, knowing it would take time, Mitch worked on that flip every day until he was eventually able to perform something that is still a state-of-the-art skill.

But if originality is the most exciting part of gymnastics, it is also often the hardest. I know it was for me, and I think that's true for the majority of gymnasts. It's difficult to be an original. Originality doesn't mean so much that you go against the grain as it means you *leave* the grain. That usually involves knocking down a few fences and departing from some of your comfort zones in the process.

Of course, gymnastics isn't the only area where originality is difficult to come by. That's true in most of the things we do. It's so much easier, and safer, to do it the way everyone else is doing it. And yet, originality is what lifts us to heights and accomplishments we otherwise couldn't have even imagined.

If at First You Don't Succeed . . . Stick with It

Originality isn't much good if you don't have faith in what you're doing. If you bail out at the first problem you won't get very far. The idea is to get a plan and stick with it. Luckily for me, Mako understood that, and over time I really came to appreciate how important it was to trust in what he was doing.

It wasn't that his way—our way—was the one and only way to achieve success. Far from it. I know other gymnasts, great champions, who had an approach entirely different from mine. Many approaches can work, as long you stay true to them.

I remember a magazine article I once read on an airline flight. This was many years ago, but it had a big impact on me. It was about successful professional sports teams. Someone had done a long-term study in an attempt to determine the keys to enduring success. At that point the top football franchises were the Raiders and Cowboys, and in baseball the Yankees and Dodgers were the model franchises. These teams didn't win the title every year, but they were always in contention, and they almost always had winning seasons. They had a resiliency. They just didn't hit bottom. Other teams would be up one year, then way down the next, like they were riding a roller coaster. But not the Raiders, Cowboys, Dodgers and Yankees. They were consistent winners.

This wasn't a sports article, but a business article, looking at the sports world to see if there might be something there to be learned.

Close examination of the successful franchises revealed a curious thing: They had almost nothing in common. In football, the Raiders and the Cowboys could hardly have been more different. The Raiders perpetuated a wild bunch image, skull and crossbones and all that. Their motto was "Just Win Baby!" The Cowboys, by contrast, were "America's Team," straight-laced (well, back then) and relatively conservative. In baseball, the Yankees and Dodgers were similarly dissimilar. One was on the West coast, the other on the East coast. Their management styles were as different as New York and L.A. They would never be confused for each other.

So the researchers had to look deeper. After getting beyond appearances and methods of operation, what they finally uncovered was this: All four of these franchises were intensely loyal to their philosophies. Dissimilar as they were, they all stuck to their plans. That was what they had in common. Other teams would change all the time, they'd replace management or they'd add this program or change that one. They were a product of their whims. One year they'd be up, the next year they'd be down. And then they'd try something else. But these consistently successful franchises didn't do that. They stuck to their plans, diverse as they were. They weren't in the business of change for change's sake, and that seemed to make the difference. They were all originals, in their own way, and they stuck fiercely to that originality.

Different Strokes

Because of environment, heredity, culture, and about a thousand other things, what works for one person may not work for another. That's another key element to being a true original. Trying to copy another person's way of doing things can often be a fast route to disappointment. There's a big difference between inspiration and duplication. What works for one person might be the exact opposite of what works for someone else. There are as many paths to success as there are people trying to get there. The ability to "think originally" is what matters. Sometimes what you think about is only going to be secondary to the new mindset it produces, one that says "I can do things my way, and I can be successful."

The Long Run

Getting in touch with our "original side" is what lets us realize how "individual" we really are. We are each of us every bit as unique as our fingerprints. Keeping that in mind allows us to transform thoughts of "Oh, what's the use, whatever I try somebody else is bound to have already thought of first," to "Even if somebody else has thought of it first, they haven't thought of it quite the way I've thought of it."

Appreciating and understanding our own individuality keeps us looking for what's around the next corner. Knowing we're all "true originals" gives us freedom to explore, to experiment. In essence, it frees us up to be ourselves.

To illustrate how this works, I'd like to cite the experiences of two great innovators—one an Olympic runner, the other an inventor.

The Olympic runner was Abebe Bikila, a distance runner from Ethiopia who won gold medals in the Olympic Games by winning the marathon in Rome in 1960 and again in Tokyo in 1964.

When Bikila arrived in Rome at the age of 28 he was a complete unknown. This was before the distance runners of middle Africa had become renowned for their capacity for endurance. In fact, no African had ever won an Olympic medal to that point in time, and few had even tried.

So when Bikila, a private in the Ethiopian Army, showed up at the starting line in Rome *without shoes,* he was nothing more than an amusement to the established international field. The race would be run along the ancient Appian Way in Rome, which meant the entire 26.2-mile distance would be covered by cobblestones. A test for the best of running shoes, let alone bare feet.

But Bikila, who'd trained for years by running barefoot around the Emperor's Palace back home in Addis Ababa (located at 8,100 feet above sea level), was undeterred. Going without shoes was his way. He never wore shoes. He was used to running in the mountains. For him, cobblestones would be a breeze. He wasn't about to wear shoes simply because it would allow him to conform to what everyone else was doing. No matter how much they stared, he didn't second guess himself when he saw everyone else in shoes.

He did know what he was up against, however, and that was the best distance runners in the world. To win would take more than bare feet and an independent nature. It would require every ounce of determination and strategy he could summon.

So Abebe Bikila did his homework. In the days before the race, he carefully went over the marathon course, memorizing its twists and turns and elevation changes. About a mile from the finish, at the start of an incline, he and his coach noted that the course went directly past the obelisk (or monument) of Axum. The obelisk's roots dated back to Rome's conquest of Axum, the ancient kingdom in northeastern Africa from which Ethiopia eventually emerged. After the Roman soldiers invaded and vanquished the natives of Axum, they returned to Rome with considerable booty, including this obelisk, which they'd happened to transplant here, along the Appian Way.

Well, every incentive in a storm, right? Abebe Bikila was no dummy. He decided that he would use the sight of that obelisk—an object of art that had been stolen from his country (even if it was thousands of years ago)—to give him a wake-up call. He reasoned that it was near enough the finish that when he saw it he would use it as a motivation to kick into his highest gear, in spite of his fatigue, and stay there until he crossed the finish line at the Arch of Constantine.

And that's exactly what he did. After breaking away from a lead group of four at the eighteen-mile mark, he and Rhadi Ben Abdesselem of Morocco ran stride for stride at a punishing five-minute-per-mile pace. The crowd assumed the heavily favored Abdesselem would eventually pull away, that the barefoot unknown from Ethiopia would crack. But with a mile to go, directly opposite the obelisk of Axum, it was the barefoot unknown, his feet still bare, his face expressionless, who turned up the pace and left his rival quickly behind. Bikila won by two hundred yards, an incredible margin over the final uphill mile. His time was a new world record.

If Abebe Bikila had been worried about appearances, or about inexperience, or about the riskiness of doing it his way, he could have easily missed his goal. But he had an original game plan and he stuck to it. He returned to his homeland as the first great African Olympic distance champion, an inspiration to millions.

Double Vision

If Abebe Bikila heard his own drummer, what about Chester Carlson?

You'd be hard pressed to name many inventions of the 20th century that have had as much impact as the copy machine. Hardly a day goes by for many people when they don't use one. It seems most people now have copiers in their own homes. To find a piece of carbon paper—which was how they used to copy documents back in the dark ages of the 1950's—you have to look in a museum. The copy machine is now a way of life around the world.

And it all came about because of a shy, retiring man named Chester Carlson, who spent much of his life in poverty, and a failing photo-supply manufacturer in Rochester, N.Y., named the Haloid Company. It was the collaboration of these two at a point when both were at the height of their struggles—looking like anything but successes—that brought about astonishing results. Their collective penchant to be "original" would change the way the world did its business.

Chester Carlson, a transplanted Californian, was out of work during the heart of the Great Depression when he landed a job in 1933 in the patent department of P. R. Mallory and Company, a New York City firm that specialized in electrical components. Carlson's job at P. R. Mallory was to prepare patent documents that conformed with government regulations, a job that called for Chester to meticulously hand-copy the documents. There was no alternative. At the time, the only way to copy documents other than by hand was either by carbon paper or by photography, and neither would do for the exacting work Carlson had to do. Day after day, he copied line after line. It was a tedious process, and especially so for Carlson, who was near-sighted.

It's small wonder that Carlson, suffering from writer's cramp and tired eyes, spent his off hours thinking about the possibilities of a duplicating machine. If he could just invent a machine that could copy documents . . .

After first conducting some research at the New York Public Library, Carlson began experiments on the kitchen stove in his small Queens apartment. He began by tinkering with heated metal plates and a sulfur coating that smelled like rotten eggs. He called the process "Electrophotography."

The experimentation was long and tedious and, by his standards (money was basically non-existent), expensive. But Carlson was determined. He persisted until he'd finally developed a crude and rather cumbersome dry-copying machine, which he tried to sell to a number of large companies, IBM and General Electric among them.

They all declined.

This was in 1939. For six long years after that, Carlson could find no buyers for "Electrophotography." He began to get discouraged. Outside of himself, no one could see much of a future for his idea; the costs of developing his crude machine into something practical and useful seemed prohibitive.

But just when he was about to lose hope, enter the Haloid Company.

Haloid was in serious danger of going out of business. Its cross-town rival in Rochester, the Eastman Kodak Company, was grabbing the lion's share of the photo-supply market. Haloid, meanwhile, was looking at bankruptcy. The company knew that if it didn't come up with some original products of its own, it was finished.

After learning of Carlson's work in a technical journal in 1946, Haloid contacted the inventor. His idea was a long shot, but what did they have to lose? The company decided to invest a quarter of its total operating budget toward developing Chester Carlson's invention.

But first, they told him they wanted to change the name. They thought "Electrophotography" was too long and awkward. A college professor suggested calling the process "Xerography," a derivative from two Greek words meaning "dry writing." Haloid liked the sound of that, especially because if they took a little English license, they could have the word begin and end with the same letter—a tactic that hadn't worked too badly for Kodak.

The word "Xerox" was coined.

Carlson moved to Rochester and, in laboratories at the Haloid plant, worked around the clock on improvements to his "Xerox" machine. Three years later, in 1949, Haloid introduced its first commercial copier, the "Xerox Model A." The machine was bulky and difficult to use, requiring a process involving fourteen different steps, and it was hardly a commercial success. But it was a start. By 1960, Haloid introduced the "Xerox 914," a machine that could quickly produce clean, clear copies at the touch of one button.

The photocopy revolution had begun. By 1966 sales of the "Xerox 914" topped $500 million a year. The Haloid Company changed its name to "Xerox" and, to this day, the words "photocopy" and "Xerox" are synonymous.

It is now estimated that more than 500 billion documents are photocopied around the earth every year. Carlson and Haloid became wealthy beyond their wildest dreams. Indeed, Chester Carlson's invention is considered one of the most successful inventions in the history of the world. Companies must constantly keep up through innovation—even Xerox, which has had its troubles of late. Regardless of that, however, Chester Carson's story is a remarkable example of originality and perseverance.

Revolutionaries

As Chester Carlson's experience illustrates, besides risking life, limb, and embarrassment, you can usually count on originality getting you a lot of grief in the beginning. Think about it. Most of the great ideas and inventions of our time have first been looked at with, if not outright scorn, at the very least mild ridicule. Name an inventor. Any inventor. The Wright Brothers. Thomas Edison. Henry Ford. Even Benjamin Franklin. All were initially looked at as if they hadn't pulled all the chairs up to the table.

How about Dick Fosbury, one of the most famous "originals" in sports history? He was almost laughed off the track when he first tried the Fosbury Flop.

Like the Gaylord Flip, the Fosbury Flop is named after its creator. Dick Fosbury was a high jumper at Oregon State University who was just one of the crowd until he decided to get original. Instead of going over the bar feet first, Fosbury decided he'd go over head first—as he called it, "flopping."

Nothing all that revolutionary about that—other than that it was totally opposite from what the rest of the world was doing.

People looked at Fosbury like he was some kind of freak. Other high jumpers wondered if he was just acting out of frustration—which, in a way, he was. He'd first turned to "flopping" as a high jumper in high school, when he struggled with the then-popular scissors style of clearing the bar. Coaches shrugged off Fosbury as a quirky kid who would come and go. His coach at Oregon State, Berny Wagner, taught him the conventional Western Roll and insisted that he work only on that technique in practice. Everywhere he went, they kept telling Fosbury to get that flop outta here.

Then along came the Olympic Games of 1968 in Mexico City, where Dick Fosbury, the only "flopper" in the field, jumped 7' 4-1/4" to not only win the gold medal but set an Olympic record in the process. He jumped almost four inches higher than the great Valery Brumel of the Soviet Union, the gold medalist and defending Olympic champion from four years before.

The sport of high jumping would never be the same. It is now virtually impossible to find a high jumper anywhere on the face of the earth who does not flop, a la Fosbury. Dick, a number of other Olympic champions, and I wrote the book *Awaken the Olympian Within* (compiled by the great swimmer John Naber). I love the title of Dick's chapter, "*Maybe you are right and everybody else is wrong.*" My wife Donna and I hosted the book-signing party at our home. I remember how awestruck I was with so many legends in my home. At one point I turned to Donna and said, "I can't believe I have the Fosbury Flop sitting on my couch!"

Improvement

Dick Fosbury's development came about only after plenty of trial and error—and constant tinkering. Originality by itself usually isn't enough—until it's refined. And then refined again. There are plenty of examples, especially, in the business world. One that I think makes the point particularly well involves an outdoor gear company that was willing to keep trying until it got it right.

One of the most respected names in American outdoor gear is L.L.Bean. But it wasn't always so. Back in 1912, when Leon Leonwood Bean first decided to go into the mail-order business and sell the hunting boots he'd invented, the result was abysmal failure. An avid hunter and fisherman in Maine, Bean had developed a kind of hybrid hunting/fishing boot with rubber soles and leather tops. In Bean's boots you could hunt *and* fish in comfort. He was proud of his invention and, confident his fellow sportsmen would also like his boots, he decided to go into business. He placed ads in outdoor publications in Maine and the surrounding New England states. He was so sure of his boot's quality that he offered a full refund if the customer wasn't completely satisfied.

That seemed like a good idea until ninety pairs of boots were returned—from the first one hundred pairs he sold.

Mr. Bean might have closed up shop then and there. A lot of people would have. But he believed in his boots. With the right improvements he felt he could work out the problems. He borrowed $400—no small sum of money in 1912—to make his boots better, and instead of discontinuing the money-back guarantees, he stuck to his offer, adopting what would become the official

L.L.Bean company sales credo: "No sale is really complete until the product is worn out, and the customer is satisfied."

Over the years the boots got better—a lot better—and so did the business, which expanded to a full line of outdoor gear as it turned into the first of America's great "customer service" companies. L.L.Bean's mail-order customers became known as the most loyal in business history. By the way, the company is still offering full money-back guarantees.

Curveballs

Just because you're original, of course, is no guarantee that your efforts might not be trumped by someone else. Your contribution could be just the breakthrough the world is looking for—so go ahead, but do it better.

Take the case of William Arthur "Candy" Cummings. You may never have heard of him, but I'll bet you've heard of his "invention."

Cummings was a pitcher in the early days of baseball. He was born in 1848 in Ware, Massachusetts, not far from the shores of the Atlantic Ocean. From skipping clam shells across the water as a boy, he developed a unique throwing motion that, when applied to a baseball, produced what is believed to be the first curve ball in history.

Cummings first used his "curving ball" while playing for the Excelsior Juniors in Brooklyn, New York as a 16-year-old, where he picked up his nickname, "Candy," which apparently was what a lot of the players thought of his pitch. By 1876, the year the National League was formed, he signed with Hartford and won 15 games and lost just 8.

But while Cummings may have had the first curve ball in history, it wasn't the best. By the 1877 season, the hitters had gotten used to his curving ball and his career nose-dived. He went

6–14 that season and was unceremoniously released, never to pitch in the big leagues again.

But, still, they put Candy Cummings in the baseball Hall of Fame in Cooperstown. With a career record of 21–22, he's the only pitcher with a losing record in the Hall of Fame. He got there for being original.

Real Goals

Originality would seem like an uncommon component in a sport that's been around as long as ice hockey. But Team Canada came to the Salt Lake Olympics on a long losing streak. Despite inventing the game and winning five of the first six Olympic hockey tournaments, Canada's last gold medal had come in the Helsinki Winter Games in 1952. Fifty years without gold for the birthplace of hockey.

There was a lot of debate about just why Canada could manage to go half a century without an Olympic hockey championship. Some people thought it was because Canada didn't take the tournament seriously enough. Others thought it might have something to do with teams from Russia/USSR practicing year-round together. Still others—and this seemed to be the most popular reason—thought it was because international rules called for a bigger rink and that reduced the value of Canada's traditional assets of physical play and superior skating and stick skills. The big rink of the international game, conventional wisdom suggested, called for a more conservative approach and considerable more defense.

Into this debate waded Wayne Gretzky, also known as The Great One, hockey's gift to the sports world, the best hockey player ever made. In the limelight of his playing career Gretzky had competed for Team Canada in Nagano in 1998, where Canada failed yet again to win the gold medal, losing in the title match to the Czechs. After his retirement as a player, Gretzky was named director of hockey for Canada, which put him in charge of Olympic hockey.

It was Gretzky who knocked conventional big-ice wisdom on its ear. Team Canada, he decided, would play to its strengths. Forget defense. Forget conservatism. In Salt Lake the Canadians would emphasize skill and speed.

Canada started slow, losing to Sweden in its first Olympic game. But momentum began to build and, by the time of the gold medal game against America, speed and skill was dominating. Gretzky's Canadians beat the United States on home ice by a 5–2 score. It was the first time the United States had lost in the Olympics at home since 1932. Gretzy's unconventional philosophy not only ended that streak, but Canada's as well.

When All Else Fails, There's Always Dumb Luck

Originality usually takes a lot of plotting, planning, and hard work. But that doesn't mean that sometimes you can't get lucky and discover something when you're not even trying. It happened to me once in gymnastics, and only once. I came up with something original, completely by accident.

It was during a competition just a few months before the Olympics. I was on the pommel horse, performing the routine I wanted to use at the Games. I felt great as the routine progressed; everything was going according to plan. My timing was on, my extension was good, my confidence was up. I was performing on my favorite event and I had high Olympic hopes for the original skill I'd developed. It came near the beginning of my routine. In this skill I went into a handstand and then, instead of jumping off the horse, I changed hands and dropped to a scissors sequence that was one of the required skills. I was confident I could count on full originality points from this skill because it was the opposite of common pommel horse procedure. The traditional thing to do out of a handstand was a dismount. The judges knew that, and they were programmed that way. Every time they'd see a handstand they'd think, OK, that's the finish, and drop their heads to start scoring the routine. It was that automatic. The first time I did the early handstand I'm sure the judge looked down at his scoring sheet thinking, "What happened to Vidmar? He just forgot his routine. He's doing a dismount! How exciting! I'll give him a 2.3." But then he looked back up, only to see I was still up there, and just like that, I had my originality points. My score consistently jumped two-tenths of a point after that—because of that skill.

On the floor that day I'd already successfully done that skill, and sailed through the rest of the routine quite smoothly afterward. All that remained was my dismount. Which is when the trouble began.

My finish called for a flare up to a one-armed handstand, and then the dismount. I'd done this maneuver thousands of times and didn't anticipate any problem now. But as I went into my handstand my grip wasn't right and my hand started to slip off the horse. If I didn't do something very quickly, the next thing to hit the horse would be my face. (I hate it when that happens.) So instead, I threw my left hand, the free one, back on the horse, used it to pivot over to the other side, and then I flipped off, landing on my feet . . . mortified.

It was a big mistake and I knew it. Instead of standing squarely on the mat and looking directly at the chief judge, I was facing the opposite side of the arena. I wasn't quite sure how I'd gotten there.

By this point I was so exasperated that I'd let a perfectly good routine slip right out of my hands—literally in this case—that the last thing I felt like doing was the obligatory turn to face and acknowledge the judge. But no routine is over until you face the judge, which in this case meant turning completely around. Fortunately, that gave me enough time to compose myself, and by the time I did an about-face and looked at the superior judge, I thought I'd take a chance. I decided to acknowledge him as if he was briefly blinded and never saw the backward dismount mistake.

I did just that. I wheeled around and faced the judge, smiling and looking extremely satisfied with myself. Pumping my fist as I left the mat, I reached Mako, who had this worried look on his face and I gave him a high-five and shouted, "Yes!" All the while I said to myself, "I can't believe I just did that!"

Out of sight, the theatrics over, Mako whispered, "What happened?!"

"I almost hit my face, that's what happened," I answered. Then, I started to complain, "Look, I've got the Olympics in three months and I'm still falling off pommel horse! I can't afford any more mistakes like this, the judges are going to kill me!" So I waited in frustration for my score . . . a 9.9.

Good score.

Excellent score.

Afterward the head judge walked over to me and said, "Hey, Pete, I really liked that new dismount. I've never seen it before."

Neither had I. But I didn't tell him that.

When he left, Mako looked at me, straight-faced, and said, "Let's use it."

So we did. For the next three months I worked and polished that move. What began as a near-fall became a full-fledged meant-to-do-it dismount. I got it down cold. In the Olympics I scored two perfect 10's on the pommel horse and won the gold medal. To be perfectly honest it wasn't just because of that dismount. It wasn't even very flashy. But every little bit helps.

Psychology

Something else I learned from Mako is the value of having people in your life who take the time to get to know you so they can understand you and treat you as an individual. I think really getting to know someone takes time and effort, and I think it's something the great teachers and coaches—and the great parents too—all do. Once you really know a person then you've put yourself in a position to know how best to help them.

People ask me if I ever had a sports psychologist and I always say no, but I had a coach.

Mako was great at psychology. He knew just the right buttons to push. When I first started gymnastics, if I complained, he wouldn't give me a lecture, he'd just launch into a story.

I remember one day in the gym when I was working out on the rings and I had torn blisters on my hand. Now, torn blisters to a gymnast is like dirt under his fingernails to a farmer. It comes with the territory. It hurts, it burns, but it's a common occurrence and no one's ever died from it.

This was toward the end of the day and I was exhausted, so the torn blisters were all the more annoying. "Wow! This hurts!" I said. I was young. I wanted sympathy. I wanted off those rings.

All Mako did was tell a story.

"Peter," he said, "did I ever tell you about the time I was competing at the national championships and at the very beginning of the ring routine I tore both my hands, from the base of the palm all the way to the base of the fingers? Complete tears. Both hands."

"Wow," I said. "Did it hurt?"

"Yeah," he said. "It really hurt bad."

"So what did you do?"

"Oh, I held on, and I won."

Then he walked away.

I hated that. It always made me mad when he did that. But then I'd chalk up my hands again and I'd think, he's not going to make fun of me like that, I'm as tough as he is, and then I'd work harder.

I remember another time when I was working out on the high bar and my wrists were so tired I could barely hang on. I made the mistake of mentioning this to Mako.

"Pete," he said, "did I ever tell you about the Kubica brothers of Poland?" (Oh no, not again.)

"No!" I said, rolling my eyes, "I've never heard of the Kubica brothers of Poland."

He proceeded to tell me about these two Polish brothers, the Kubicas, and how he walked up to one of them once at a meet to shake hands. Mako looked down and noticed that he only had three fingers on his right hand. He said, "And he was a great high bar man."

Then he walked away—I counted five fingers on each of my hands and I kept working out.

That kind of psychology wouldn't work for everyone, but Mako knew it worked for me. He never had to tell me "work harder," or "don't be a wimp," he'd just tell me a story. For nearly a dozen years, he told me his stories.

He had credibility also. He talked the talk *and* walked the walk. This is a man who is over fifty and still works out religiously. I ask him, why do you do it? And he says that it's who he is, and, besides, he needs to be an example to those he coaches.

"If I'm over fifty and keep getting stronger," he asks, "how can somebody who's twenty-two and in college say that they can't get any stronger?"

That's effective coaching. That's why Dan Gable, the Olympic champion who set the record for national wrestling championships at the University of Iowa, was such a great wrestling coach. People say Dan Gable could beat many of his wrestlers because he would work out with them and wrestle with them. When a coach, a leader, is willing to endure the same hardships, the same discipline, the same pain, as his students—within reason, of course—then that person is going to gain more and more respect. It's not some overweight sergeant saying, "Drop and give me fifty pushups," it's a guy who will drop and do the fifty with you.

Incentive, Incentive, Incentive

The main reason I don't agree with the discontinuance of the R.O.V. method of gymnastics judging—and the reason why I'd like to see its return—is because it takes away that compelling need to be original. With no R.O.V., they've taken away the mandate for originality, and without that mandate it's too easy to stay with the status quo, and become a formula. Risk and virtuosity don't suffer as much with the degree-of-difficulty scoring that's now in place. The top skills are risky by nature and performances done with style and virtuosity are always going to be recognized.

But originality needs constant encouragement. It needs a *reason*. Otherwise, it's too tempting to stick with what's tried and true.

Incentive has to come from somewhere. And while we'd all like to think we're perfectly capable of inspiring ourselves toward originality, usually it's external influences that have the greatest and the quickest effect. It's amazing how inventive we can get when the situation demands it.

Virtuosity

---

virtuosity 2. *great technical skill in some fine art.*

WEBSTER'S

"Virtue is reason which has become energy."

FRIEDRICH SCHLEGEL

"I'll do my best—I can do no less."

ERIC LIDDELL IN *CHARIOTS OF FIRE*

AFTER DECIDING NOT TO JUMP in the river, my next thought was more rational.

But not much more.

Recall that night in Budapest when I fell off the high bar in the world championships—the fateful "turning point" night I've already detailed in the chapter on Risk? Well, once I'd decided I wasn't going to take risky skills for granted anymore, my next thought was this: *From now on, I'm going to work twice as hard.*

Never again was I going to fail from lack of effort. I was never going to stop working. I would be indefatigable. If the next guy worked out eight hours a day, I would double that. I'd work out sixteen.

Nothing wrong with that sort of thinking, of course, other than that it was impossible.

How many times have you heard a parent or a coach or a teacher say the "you're going to have to work twice as hard" line?

"You better study twice as hard if you're going to get better grades."

"You better train twice as hard if you want to be on this team."

"You better practice the piano twice as long if you want to be the best at the recital."

And so on.

The sentiment makes sense, but the math doesn't. The fact of the matter is, most of the time, no matter how much we might want to, it's not humanly possible to double any significant effort. It's certainly not possible in the case of a world-class athlete. Any gymnast hoping to make the Olympics is going to be working out at least six hours a day. That's minimum. So if I'm going to double that, I have to train twelve hours a day. Technically, that may be possible, but from a physical standpoint it makes no sense. It would be exhausting to the point of being counterproductive. My body would fall apart from the strain.

The key, of course, isn't to work twice as hard, but just a fraction harder, or smarter, or longer. In the end, it's the fractions that matter. Concentrate just a little more. Work out just a little longer. Increase the quality of your training bit by bit.

Being the best is rarely a matter of being twice as good as anyone else. It's usually measured by tenths of seconds and fractions of inches.

In the Olympic arena, I can give you example after example. Connie Carpenter-Phinney won the women's road racing gold medal in cycling in the 1984 Olympics by one inch—after fifty miles of racing. Matt Biondi lost the 100-meter butterfly final in the 1988 Olympics in Seoul by one-hundredth of a second.

Remember Mary Lou Retton in the 1984 Games in Los Angeles? She won her gold medal in the women's all-around with a dramatic 10 on the vault. She was perfect. And do you know what she needed to win? That's right, a perfect 10. A 9.9 wouldn't have been good enough. She won by five-hundredths of a point. When Casey Fitzrandolph won the 500-meter speed skating gold in Salt Lake City, *eighth* place was only six-hundredths of a second behind!

No one wins by running twice as fast or jumping twice as far or scoring twice as many points as the next guy. This is so obvious it's almost offensive. We win by fractions. By inches. By portions of seconds undetected to the naked eye. Take any Olympic champion and ask what made him or her the best. Did they work twice as hard? Were they twice as dedicated? The answer will be no. The same is true in any profession or pursuit.

There was an interesting article published a few years ago in *Sports Illustrated*. The author was George Plimpton and he told a story about a phenomenal new rookie playing baseball for the New York Mets named Hayden "Sidd" Finch. Sidd Finch, Plimpton reported, was a pitcher who could throw a baseball 168 miles an hour. That was a third faster than anybody in the major leagues; a third faster, in fact, than anyone had ever thrown a baseball in history. The fastest time ever recorded by a radar gun was 104 miles an hour. This guy could throw 64 miles an hour faster than that.

Plimpton reported that Finch was proving to be unhittable in spring training. The Mets' best hitters were going up to the plate and not swinging until the ball was already in the catcher's mitt.

They couldn't even *see* the pitch. According to Plimpton, Finch was a Harvard graduate who studied Eastern religions and was rumored to have spent time in Tibet where he was influenced by Tibetan monks. He had an unorthodox pitching delivery, throwing with his arm completely stiff—and he wore hiking boots instead of baseball cleats.

"It's possible that an absolute superpitcher is coming into baseball," Plimpton wrote, "so remarkable that the delicate balance between pitcher and hitter could be turned into disarray. He may well change the course of baseball history."

Sidd Finch and his 168-mph fastball may indeed have changed the course of baseball history. Except for one detail. He did not exist. Plimpton's article appeared in the April 1st edition of *Sports Illustrated.* He made the whole thing up. It was all an elaborate April Fool's joke, which the magazine revealed in its following issue.

There was no phenom/mystic named Sidd Finch who threw baseballs as if they were BB's. The Mets weren't shoo-ins for the pennant and the World Series. The joke was on the readers.

The possibility was intriguing, however. What if a person really could perform a third above the rest? What would be the impact? It's easy to imagine that such a performer really could change the course of any sport's history.

But in the normal scheme of things, it just doesn't work that way. Not only can't we throw twice—or even a third—as fast as everyone else, or jump twice as high as others, we can't work twice as hard, either.

Little by Little

When I made the 1984 Olympic team along with Mitch Gaylord and Tim Daggett, I knew I couldn't outwork them by very much, if at all. We'd been teammates at UCLA for four years and I knew how hard they went at it. In college I had a more modest goal and it was this: I'd be the last person out of the gym every single day.

Now that was pretty hard to do when not only Mitch and Tim, but the rest of the team as well, had that same goal. Workouts used to get really long. But every once in a while I'd actually make my goal. At the end of the day, I'd find myself in an empty gym by myself. I'd work an extra fifteen or twenty minutes and feel like I was gaining ground.

I once calculated just how much of a difference fifteen extra minutes a day could make. If you did that every day for a year it would add up to ninety-one more hours of training. Think of the benefits if that training were applied to those skills that needed a little extra attention. For an athlete training three hours a day, fifteen extra minutes a day over a year adds up to an extra month of training.

That's what develops virtuosity.

Virtuosity is what you get when you combine the practical results of hard work, mixing it in with extra effort and blending it all with enthusiasm and passion.

Virtuosity is taking the same skill everybody does—and doing it better.

In music a *virtuoso* is one who displays great skill in his or her presentation. In gymnastics virtuosity means doing a skill with more amplitude, more extension, more artistry—performing with such style that, when a judge looks at a skill he's seen a hundred times, he stops and says, "Wow, I've seen that done before but I like it done *like that*."

That's virtuosity. And for the most part it's the result of long, hard, painstaking, dedicated work. Work that can often be boring and is almost always repetitive. The route to real virtuosity is a long, hard climb, with few shortcuts.

The challenge is to stay focused while on the climb.

We've all been there. I know I've been there. I've been midway through workouts and thought I'd go out of my mind from the boredom, and yet I've known I couldn't afford to stop. I'd know if I did something on the pommel horse a thousand times with as much focus and attention as I did the very first time, I'd be a better gymnast. That's what I needed to do if I wanted to get a fraction of an edge over the competition. That was, and always will be, the challenge: To keep up the focus, the enthusiasm, the effort, even when it's a long day, even when I'm extra-tired and not as inspired as I need to be.

We can all be focused—when we feel like it. The hard part is staying focused when we don't feel like it; when it's just plain inconvenient to put forth the effort. Those are the times that give us the opportunity to develop virtuosity.

Dedication

Whenever and wherever you find true virtuosity, look behind the scenes and "consistency" and "commitment" will be there every time. They are the keys to virtuosity.

A consistent effort is necessary to achieve any worthwhile goal, and it's commitment that drives consistency. When we're committed to the cause, whatever it might be, we'll be willing to endure not just boredom but injury and illness and bad luck and a thousand other obstacles that could otherwise halt us in our tracks.

By the time of my big fall in Budapest, I'd luckily been well prepared mentally. As usual, my coach was several jumps—and years—ahead of me. Several years earlier he'd done something that seemed rather inane at the time, but ended up instilling in me much more mental toughness than I'd have ever managed otherwise. Only with the clarity of hindsight can I look back and see the great value of an experience that allowed me to be committed and, hence, develop consistency.

It was in the summer of 1979 and things were going very well in my training. I was at the U.S. Olympic Festival, which was held that year on the campus of the United States Air Force Academy in Colorado Springs. I was on my way to a fifth-place finish that would pave the way for my qualifying for my first world championship team. Every morning before that day's competition I would meet Mako in the middle of the quad in the center of the campus. It's a huge quad, surrounded by the campus and the Rocky Mountains beyond—a very inspiring setting all by itself.

Mako and I would run around the quad in that thin mountain air, always finishing with a short, fast sprint. (I enjoyed racing Mako—sprinting was the one thing I could beat him at. I could blow him away.) After running we'd do some stretches and some exercises and go over our routine for the day. Then we'd have breakfast.

About midway through the week Mako looked at me and said, "Pete, do you know what a vow is?"

Whenever Mako asked questions I'd get nervous. I knew he always had a motive behind them, and that motive usually involved more work for me.

"A what?" I said. I guess I was buying time.

"A vow," he said.

"Yeah," I answered. "I know what a vow is."

"Let's make a vow," he said. "Let's vow that you will do morning training before breakfast every day like this until you graduate from college. And I will too."

So what was I going to say? No?

"Uh, OK," I said.

"Let's shake on it."

So we shook on it, and when we did, when I shook his hand, even though there was no drum roll, no trumpets blaring and no lawyers were writing it down, I knew it was binding. I thought, "I have to do this." Which was great at the time. I was 18 years old. I was having the best meet of my life. I was fired up.

But I hadn't even *started* college yet.

Keeping that vow was a piece of cake for the first couple of months, when I was healthy, when I didn't have any early classes. And even after I started my freshman year at UCLA that fall, and I did have early classes, it wasn't that tough at first. But I knew it wouldn't always be easy to keep that vow, and I was right. It's not easy when you've blown your ankle out the day before at practice, so you can't even run, you can't even walk, and even to try that is stupid because you should be resting the ankle. It's not easy when you're tired and sore and you're behind in your homework.

I can remember being sick with the flu and doing the morning run barely moving. I can remember doing it in pouring rain. I did it when I had a fever and the very worst thing I could have done was get out of bed, and yet I got out of bed, more than once, and did that workout. Every morning. Six days every week. (Sundays off). Warmup, stretch, do something productive. That was the deal. If I slept in, I'd miss class if I had to, but I'd get that workout in. Even when I was on an airplane I'd work out before breakfast. That was probably tougher than being sick. I remember being on an overseas airplane going to an international meet, and waking up and looking over and seeing Mako doing pushups in the aisle. People were looking at him like he was nuts. I'd think, "This is so embarrassing," but I'd get down and do *my* pushups.

I never missed a day. I'd made a commitment and I was going to stick with it, NO MATTER WHAT. I had to.

It didn't make sense at times. Sometimes it was physiologically the wrong thing to do too. Sometimes I'd just be making myself worse. But that only applied to the physical side of things. Keeping that vow made me so much tougher in my mind. Psychologically it was always the right thing to do. It made me think I could handle anything.

Three of the best competitions of my life—leading up to the Olympics—were when I was ill or injured. I know I was able to compete and do my best because I'd been programmed to *Just Do It*—no matter what. All three were important meets that helped my Olympic development, and in each one, if I'd wanted to, I could have bailed out with a perfectly legitimate excuse.

The first of these "learning experiences" came at the world championships in 1981 in Moscow. This was the year after the Olympics had been held in Moscow—the Games the Americans didn't attend. Well, here it was, a year later, and we were all finally together in Russia. To say the least, that made the meet all the more interesting. It was kind of like they'd rolled the Olympics and the world championships all into one.

As Americans, it was no surprise that we weren't very popular. It was our country that had led fifty other countries away from the Moscow Games. I think they took it out on us by the food they served. (At least that's what I think.) We stayed at the Sport Hotel in Moscow and they had a fixed menu that rotated every three days. So every third day you got exactly what you'd had three days before, breakfast, lunch and dinner. That got a little monotonous, but the worst part was that the food just didn't sit well with most of us on the U.S. team. We weren't used to it. We had to bring in some cases of American food, mostly canned food, so we'd have something that felt better on our stomachs.

After a couple of weeks of that diet I was not in the best of shape. I got the flu. I was nauseous and weak and achy all over.

Of course, by now it was time for the finals, and they weren't about to postpone anything until I got feeling better. So when my name was called I did the only thing I could do—I competed.

I ended up scoring a 58.4 in the all-around, which worked out to a 9.75 average per event. That placed me thirteenth in the world, which was great for me at that stage of my development. I hadn't expected to do that well. I was very pleased. It was a real confidence booster. I scored the highest all-around total of my life—and it came amid hostile conditions, bad food, and the flu.

A couple of years after that, about a year before the L.A. Games, we had a dual meet with the Soviets in Los Angeles. They'd just completed the Gersten Pavilion on the campus of

Loyola-Marymount University, which was to be used for weightlifting in the Olympics, and they wanted to inaugurate the arena with a major international event. We were it. The Soviets, who at that point planned to attend the L.A. Olympics (they wound up returning the boycott favor), brought in all their big guns and so did we. We assembled basically the same team that would compete in the Games the next summer. They had Alexander Dityatin, who was the Olympic all-around champion in Moscow in 1980; and Yuri Korolev, the all-around champion at the 1981 world championships that were held in Moscow; and 17-year-old phenom, Dima Belozerchev, who later that year would become the youngest world all-around champion ever. The Soviets fielded a formidable team, to say the least.

Just like in Moscow, food was again my downfall on the eve of a big event. After eating dinner at our hotel the night before the meet I came down with food poisoning. This was the real thing. Anyone who's been there knows the feeling. My greatest fear was that I *wouldn't* die.

I went to my room in the hotel and, with the exception of when I threw up, stayed flat in bed. I couldn't move. I didn't want to move. Mark Caso, my old UCLA buddy, was my roommate and the USA team alternate. I kept telling him, "You're going to have to compete for me. I can't move." Finally I asked Mark to go get Mako, who, besides being my personal coach, was an assistant coach for the U.S. team.

Mako walked in and with his customary bedside manner said, "So, Pete, you're really sick huh?"

"Yeah," I said, "I've been throwing up all night. I can't move."

"Wow," he said. "Well, don't eat until you feel like you might be hungry. Listen to your body and tonight just do the best you can."

As he left I thought, "Did he say what I think he said? This isn't just nerves because it's the Russians. Can't he see I can't even move? I can't even do a dismount from my bed!"

I looked at Mark and said, "I can't believe he thinks I can compete tonight!"

I stayed in bed the whole day. That evening I put my uniform on, positive that once I got to the arena they'd see I was too sick to compete and replace me with Mark. I was worn out. I hadn't eaten anything all day and I'd thrown up everything the night before.

But the bus ride wasn't as bad as I thought it would be, and after I got to the arena and started stretching, the nausea began to leave. I started feeling normal again. I was getting better. That was the good news. The bad news was that I was famished. I needed fuel fast. And there wasn't any real food around. They had concession stands with chili dogs and popcorn and drinks and that was it.

So I ran to the back of a concession stand and asked the guy if he could give me a 7-Up and three or four hotdog buns. I was going for straight carbohydrates. The Russians must have thought I had the most bizarre gymnastics warmup routine in the world. I'd do a tumbling pass, then I'd grab a hotdog bun and shove it down my throat. It'd eat it, swallow it, drink a little of the 7-Up, set it down, rest for a minute, and then do another tumbling pass. I'd go to the pommel horse and do the same thing.

Then the competition began and I had the meet of my life. I ended up tying Yuri Korolev, the defending world champion, for the all-around title. *Wide World of Sports* was there and taped the whole thing. It was a significant step for me, and made a big difference in my career. But if I had established a habit of copping out, of not competing unless I was at my best, I wouldn't have even tried that night. I'd have watched that meet back at the hotel, in bed.

Even more significant, in terms of my personal Road to the Olympics, it was my final meet before the '84 Games. This was in Jacksonville, Florida, where the U.S. Gymnastics Federation held that year's U.S. Olympic trials.

Since my fall from the high bar in Budapest, everything had gotten back on track. I knew I was in the best shape of my life. I knew I'd taken time to work on my weaknesses. My confidence was at an all-time high. But about a week before the Trials I tore a capsule in my ankle. It was a small tear below the tibia in my right leg. No big deal overall, except for one thing. The tear happened to be located at the exact point in the ankle that takes all the pressure when you finish a routine AND LAND PERFECTLY. That's the object of any routine, of course. A perfect landing. Legs slightly bent, knees forward, ankles parallel. That's how you want to finish. When you do it just right, the achilles tendon takes most of the strain, which explains why some gymnasts are always stretching their achilles.

Now, no matter how much I stretched, I found that when I landed just right it felt as if someone was stabbing a sharp knife into my ankle. I'd get this single, sharp, bolting pain that would cause me to pull my leg straight in the air.

This was not good. At the trials, either you come through or you don't. No matter what credentials you might have, no matter if you've won every major championship over the past decade, if you don't cut it there you don't go to the Olympics. Period. And here I was with this problem. If I landed backward, if I took a step back, I was fine. Forward. Same thing. Any landing that took pressure off the ankle was no problem. The only thing that hurt was a perfect landing—the end-all goal of gymnastics.

I remember Mako going to Abe Grossfeld, our head coach, the day of the meet and asking, "What if Peter doesn't finish his floor routine today? He's hurt his ankle." Abe looked at him incredulously and said, "What do you mean, he's hurt his ankle! He's got to finish his floor routine!"

So I did the only thing my instincts would let me do. On my first tumbling pass, a roundoff to a back handspring, full twisting double back flip, I came down and landed perfectly. I mean

I stuck it. It was there, and I just couldn't refuse. For a split second all I felt was the emotional satisfaction. A dead solid perfect landing. Yesssssssss!

That was quickly followed by Wowwwwwwwwwww! That hurt!

The pain was incredible. It was all I could do not to cry out in front of the judges. At that point, my old perfectionist instincts gave way to my new instincts not to hurt myself.

On my next pass, no matter how much I didn't want to, I landed just a little off-center. I couldn't help it. It's amazing, the brakes your body will apply to keep you from hurting yourself. I made myself keep landing as close to dead-center as I could, instead of pulling out too much, but it wasn't easy—and it sure wasn't perfect.

Luckily, I came close enough on those landings to not only make the Olympic team, but to win the trials as well.

With the help of a cortisone shot and some fortunate timing I was able to compete thirty days later in the Olympics with no ankle pain (although the pain did return three days after the end of the Games). But thank goodness I was able to make it through the trials in spite of the pain. If I hadn't had effective mental preparation prior to the trials, I would have been out of the Olympics before the Olympics ever got started. And you would still be reading some book by an ex-baseball player.

For Good Reason

At the core of commitment (and virtuosity) is value. That's what kept me competing when I was sick or injured. I applied enough value to what I was doing so that I was willing to pay the price.

When we decide something *is worth it*, we'll be willing to suspend fatigue, inconvenience, hardship, even safety. And when we decide something isn't worth it, we won't. In short, value is what fuels incentive. Value provides the reason "why."

To illustrate this, pretend that you're standing in front of a balance beam—you've seen a balance beam in women's gymnastics. It's a solid beam about four inches wide and about twenty feet long. Usually it's on a stand that's a few feet off the floor.

But we've taken the legs off so the balance beam is just laying there on the ground. Now, you're at one end of the beam and I'm at the other. I've got a hundred dollar bill in my hand and it's yours if you walk across the beam to get it from me. Would you do it? Would you try to walk across that four-inch wide beam? Of course you would. We all would. Piece of cake.

Now let's change a few of the variables. Let's take that same beam to the Grand Canyon. We'll place it on the edge of the famous North Rim, so that it extends across the canyon to the other side. The Colorado River is a few thousand feet below. We'll even bolt the beam down. So relax, it won't move.

It's the same beam and the same deal. I'm standing on one end with a hundred dollar bill in my hand. It's yours if you'll walk across the beam to get it. Would you do it now? Of course you wouldn't. You'd be crazy to risk that fall for a hundred dollars, even if you've already demonstrated you're perfectly capable of walking the length of that beam without falling off.

What if I up the ante? How about ten thousand dollars? Walk across and it's all yours. How about a million dollars? Still no deal? Why not? Because of the sudden deceleration at the end of the fall should you happen to slip?

The point is, sometimes you decide it's worth it and sometimes you decide it isn't. It's a value judgment.

But let's add one more twist to the scenario.

I'm not standing at the end of the beam waving money any longer. In my place is a bad guy and he's standing there holding your five-year-old child, or your five-year-old grandchild. If you don't walk across the beam he's going to let the child go.

Would you walk across the beam now? You bet you would (and the bad guy better not be there when you get there, right?).

What changed? Why are you now willing to do something you wouldn't have done for a million dollars? Because now there's something on the other end of that beam that makes it worth it to cross, that's why. It may not be a pleasant experience. It may be a horrible experience, as a matter of fact. But it matters. There's value on the other end. (I've found that this example works well in front of a live audience when I ask for the response from parents of young children. It doesn't work as well for the parents of teenagers!)

The exact same task—crossing the beam—can look completely different to us depending on our motivation (the value we see attached to the other end). When the difficulty factor increases, it's vital to keep the value on the other end of the beam in focus.

Mind Games

In training for the Olympics, when I first walked into the gym and was fresh and rested, it wasn't difficult to talk myself into working hard. The Olympics were coming. I was anxious. I was excited. I was ready. It was easy to get started. It was easy to want to cross the imaginary beam. It was as if the beam were sitting flat on the ground.

But at the end of the workout, when I was tired and quickly running out of energy, it always got more difficult. Even though the task I was doing at the end of the day was often identical to what I'd been doing at the beginning of the day, now that fatigue and boredom had entered the picture, it always looked more difficult. In my eyes the beam wasn't on the floor any more. It was way up there. If I couldn't focus on why I needed to cross it, I probably wouldn't.

If there is one thing I learned by observing other athletes, it's this: Everyone works hard when they feel like it, when they're having a good day, when they get results, especially instant results. But the best (and I was lucky that I was able to train with the best) are able to focus when they don't feel like it any more; when it's just plain inconvenient to put forth the effort.

Anyone in sales knows the last client or customer at the end of a long tiring day is just as important as the first customer at the beginning of the day, but it's harder to give the same attention and care to that last customer.

My daily training partner at UCLA and, after that, on the United States Olympic team, was my best friend, Tim Daggett. These days, any fan of the Olympics knows Tim as NBC's gymnastics commentator at the Olympic Games and other events.

Every day Tim and I would walk into the gym, ready to go, fired up, and every day by the end of the workout we'd be running on empty, just trying to hang on. The goal in gymnastics is perfection, and the key to perfection is repetition. We would perform each routine on each piece of apparatus over and over again. But repetitions have a way of wearing you down. When we were gearing up for the Olympics, we increased our number of routines and that made it all the more difficult to stay focused.

We'd do our best to keep each other going. There are six events in men's gymnastics and we'd take turns acting as head cheerleader. We'd start out on the floor exercise and do our planned routines there. Then we'd go to the pommel horse, the best event for both of us, and we'd go over our routines and then go over them again. Then it was off to the rings and more of the same. *Come on, come on,* we'd keep saying, *the Olympics are coming, we've got to keep working.*

On we'd continue. From rings to vault. Slam the board, do vault after vault . . . after . . . vault . . . the . . . Olympics . . . are . . . soon. Then to the parallel bars. Go over the routines, and then go over them again.

By the time we'd get to the last event, the high bar, we'd invariably be less excited about what we were doing than when we'd started. By now we'd have been in the gym for five or six hours. We're tired. We've had enough. No matter how hard we've tried to keep ourselves psyched, we're running down. Ankles are swollen, blisters are torn, shoulders hurt. . . . But we couldn't afford to quit and we knew it.

It was often at this time at the end of the day, in an empty gym that I would stop and ask Tim these questions. "Hey Tim," I'd say, "why are we here? What are we doing this for? What's the goal? Is that goal still worth working for *right now*?"

So we used to close with this little fantasy ritual that was intended to short-circuit our brains. And most of the time, it worked.

We'd imagine ourselves actually competing in the Olympic Games. And not just competing sometime during the meet, but at the conclusion, when all the pressure was on, and the outcome was . . . up . . . to . . . us.

We'd imagine the ultimate gymnastics scenario and put ourselves smack in the middle of it.

We all know what the ultimate experience is in baseball, right? Tie game in the seventh game of the World Series, each team with three wins apiece, bottom of the ninth inning, two outs, down by three runs, bases loaded, full count, you're at the plate . . . and you hit that ball out of the park. I mean, that's got to be the ultimate in baseball (the worst baseball experience would simultaneously be occurring to the pitcher). Take any baseball player and promise him that situation, that chance, that opportunity, and then ask him if that's worth working for right now, and what will he say? Yes. Absolutely. You bet it is. Because if he imagines himself in that bottom-of-the-ninth situation with the bat in his hands, he's going to want to come through. He's going to want to hit that grand slam.

Well, we imagined the same thing in gymnastics. The ultimate scenario. I'd say, "OK, Tim, let's just imagine it's the

Olympic Games. Men's gymnastics team finals. U.S. team on its last event of the night. Just happens to be the high bar. The last two guys up for the United States are Tim Daggett and Peter Vidmar. Our team is neck-and-neck with the People's Republic of China, the reigning world champions, and we have to hit our routines perfectly to win the Olympic team gold medal."

At that point we'd be thinking, "Yeah, right. We're never going to be neck and neck with those guys. They were Number One at the Budapest world championships (where I had my un-planned departure from the high bar). We didn't even win a medal. *It's not going to happen.*"

But what if? How would we feel? How would we come through?

So I'd walk over, chalk up my hands, close my eyes, and, in this now-empty gym at the end of a long day, visualize an Olympic arena with thirteen thousand people in the seats and another two hundred million watching me live on television. In my mind I had this one chance to perform my routine, and if I make it we win the gold medal. If I don't, we lose.

My heart starts to pound.

Now, I'm not tired any more.

First, I'd be the announcer. I'd cup my hands around my mouth, and say, "Next up, from the United States of America, Tim Daggett. . . ." Then Tim would go through his routine as if it were the *real thing.*

Then Tim would go over to the corner of the gym, cup his hands around his mouth, and in his best announcer-voice say, "Next up, from the United States of America, Peter Vidmar."

Now it was my turn and I'd get ready to start. But I wouldn't begin just when I wanted to. In a real competition you start only after the judge gives you the signal by raising his hand and the green light goes on. Waiting for that green light can be very unnerving. Trent Dimas won the gold medal for the United States in the 1992 Olympics on the high bar and he had to wait six minutes before the light went on. There was a disagreement over the previous score and all he could do was stand there while the judges argued. In the Los Angeles Games Julianne McNamara had to stand before the beam for nine and a half minutes for the same reason. That's an eternity under the circumstances. Worse than waiting for Tonya Harding to fix her skate lace.

Finally, after letting me squirm a while, Tim would shout out "Green light!" and I'd look at the superior judge, who was usually Mako. I'd raise my hand and he'd raise his right back. Then I'd turn, face the bar, grab hold, and begin my routine.

If it went fine, my day was made. I felt great. If it didn't go fine, if I didn't hit my routine, if I fell apart, or fell from the high bar, I felt miserable. I'd imagine someone from ABC Sports walking up to me with a microphone and asking, "Well, Pete, you just lost the Olympics for your whole country. How do you feel?"

Day after day we ended our workouts that way. Competing in the Olympics was a regular occurrence. We did it hundreds of times. But we knew, realistically, that it would never actually happen. Not in real life.

Well, a funny thing happened on July 21st, 1984.

This Is *Not* a Test

It was the Olympic Games, men's gymnastics team finals in Pauley Pavilion on the UCLA campus. The thirteen thousand seats were filled and a television audience in excess of two hundred million around the world was tuned in. The United States team was on its last event of the night, the high bar. The last two guys up for the United States just happened to be Tim Daggett and Peter Vidmar.

And here was the catch—our team is neck-and-neck with the People's Republic of China, and we have to hit our routines perfectly to win the gold medal. If we hit our high bar routines, we win the gold medal. Fantasy and fact had just merged into one.

Well, there are six gymnasts per team and on every event the best five scores count. That gives every team a safety valve, a score to throw out. On the high bar, we assumed we'd already used ours. Scott Johnson, our trusty leadoff man who hadn't missed a routine for two days, was heading for a perfect record until his high bar dismount. On a maneuver called a triple fly-away, which calls for three flips backward before he hits the ground, he pulled up about three degrees too soon on the third flip and slipped enough that his hand touched the floor. We assumed that that would be the score we'd throw out.

So now we were working without a net.

Jim Hartung, Scott's teammate from the University of Nebraska, went next, and the man who never made a mistake didn't make one this time, either. He did a great job, and after sticking his dismount he ran straight over to me. Why he singled me out, shouting above the crowd, I don't know, but he did. "Hey Pete," he shouted, "don't worry about it man, it's not that bad up there, just relax, just enjoy yourself. Have a good time!"

He was happy because he was done!

The judges gave him a 9.8, an excellent score. We were back on track.

Bart Conner was next. Six months after having surgery to repair a torn biceps tendon and remove forty bone chips from his elbow, he did a flawless routine with a perfect landing on the dismount. Bart scored a 9.9.

Now it was Mitch Gaylord's turn, the man the Gaylord Flip was named after. Mitch let go of the bar, flipped over the bar, and caught it perfectly, and later stuck his landing. Another successful flight. I thought he was perfect. The judges thought he was close. They gave him a 9.95.

Now came Tim Daggett's turn. You should see the film of his routine. It was incredible. He had a couple of combinations he'd invented himself and he showed those off, and then he dismounted with a double layout with a full twist, which means he didn't see the ground till it hit him. He landed perfectly. The judges agreed. He *was* perfect. They gave him a 10.

Then it was my turn.

Remember, five scores count, and if you added the scores for the five routines already completed by Scott, Jim, Bart, Mitch and Tim, that was already enough for the gold medal. No kidding. The competition wasn't yet over. I still had my high bar routine and the Chinese had two performers, Li Ning and Tong Fei, remaining on their last event, floor exercise. But even if I scored a zero and Ning and Fei both scored perfect 10's they'd couldn't catch us. Tim's 10 had made sure of that. With Tim's 10 we had just secured the U.S.A.'s first Olympic team gymnastics gold medal since the 1904 Olympic Games in St. Louis, a Games in which the gymnastics competition included wooden club juggling, long jump, and shot put! So just like we'd planned, he had won the Games! It was mathematically impossible for us to be caught.

Peter Vidmar could fall off that high bar a hundred times and the United States men's team would still be Olympic champion. We'd done it. We'd locked up the title.

But I didn't know that.

No one told me. Some of my teammates and coaches, who had done some quick calculating, knew the score and were already starting to celebrate, but I was oblivious to all that. I was standing at attention, waiting for the green light to go on so I could salute the head judge, have him salute me, and get on with the business of settling just who was going to win the gold medal. Would it be the U.S.A. or the Chinese? I thought it was up to me.

I looked at Mako, my coach for the past twelve years. As focused as ever, he simply said, "OK, Peter, let's go. You know what to do. You've done it a thousand times, just like every day back in the gym. Let's just do it one more time and let's go home. You're prepared."

And he was right. I was prepared. I hadn't waited until it was too late to figure out what I'd do if I ever found myself in a situation like this. I'd planned for this moment. I'd plotted for it and imagined what I would do. So much so that now, instead of standing in the Olympic arena with thirteen thousand people in the stands and two hundred million on television, in my mind I was able to put myself back at the UCLA gym at the end of the day with two people left in the gym. I was able to take that imaginary beam and position it where *I* wanted it. And right now, where I wanted it was lowered right back down to the floor.

When the announcer said, "From the United States of America, Peter Vidmar," I imagined it was my buddy Tim Daggett saying it, and when the green light came on I imagined that it wasn't really a green light, but that was Tim too, shouting "Green light!" And when I raised my hand toward the superior judge from East Germany (a real friendly face, especially since the athletes from his homeland had boycotted and stayed home), in my mind I was signaling my coach just like I'd signaled him every day at the end of hundreds of workouts.

In the gym, I always imagined I was at the Olympic finals. At the Olympic finals, I imagined I was back in the gym.

I turned, faced the bar, jumped up and grabbed on. I began a routine that I had done day after day after day during workouts.

I knew what I had to do and so that's what I did. I was in memory mode, going yet again where I'd already gone. I quickly made it past that risky double release move that had harpooned my chances at the world championships. I moved smoothly through the rest of routine, aware but not aware. My dismount was solid.

The judges gave me a 9.95.

Overkill.

A half hour later, the gold medals were officially ours. They draped them around our necks and played the national anthem as the Stars and Stripes was raised to the top of the arena. It was a moment we all had dreamed about, standing at attention and listening to the anthem after winning the gold medal, but still couldn't really believe was actually happening. I was breathing so fast that I started to hyperventilate on the stand, which is kind of ironic when you think about it. I was OK doing the gymnastics; it was the standing at attention that unnerved me. Some things you can't effectively imagine until they actually happen. Others, thankfully, you can.

You Win Some . . .

Winning that team gold medal was the culmination of a dream, but for a very good reason we had to keep the celebrating in check.

Two days later, some of us had to do it all over again.

Not as a team, but each on his own, as we moved on to the individual finals that would decide the Olympic champion in the all-around competition, plus each of the six men's individual events. Coming out of the team portion of the competition, I was leading the all-around and I'd also qualified for the finals in floor exercise, pommel horse, rings, and high bar. I was fourth on parallel bars and would have participated in those finals as well, but the rules only allowed for two gymnasts per country in the finals. Both Mitch and Bart were ahead of me.

So there was still plenty of work to do and now I was essentially on my own. The waiting only intensified the pressure. It was like getting to the seventh inning of a baseball game and then telling the players, OK, let's stop for a couple of days and then we'll come back and finish the game.

Internationally, I'd never been in this position before. I'd never gone into the all-around finals ahead of the likes of China's Li Ning and Japan's Koji Gushiken. I must admit, the reality of where I stood took me somewhat by surprise. I couldn't say I hadn't been warned. Mako had pulled me aside about a month before the Games and told me he thought I could win the Olympic all-around gold medal. He said I could contend with the best in the world. Mako wasn't one for false praise, so what he said should have carried a lot of weight with me, and yet that had been quite a stretch for my imagination and I'd mostly ignored it. For all the trust I had in my coach, and even after twelve years of intensive year-round training, I had a hard time imagining myself on that top-of-the-world level.

Now he could say I told you so, and I was left to wish I'd had the sense to listen better. If I had, I'm sure it would have helped not only my confidence, but also my preparation for the position I was now in. Unlike on the high bar in the team finals, in the all-around individual finals I wasn't visiting a place I'd already visually visited many times before.

But even if I hadn't spent a lot of time visualizing the position I was now in, I still had my training to lean on. And I *had* been trained, make no mistake. *I* was the culmination of that training. Again, that's where virtuosity comes from. You don't invent virtuosity because "suddenly there's a gold medal on the line and you sure could use some right about now." You've either developed it over time—or you haven't.

I'd spent the better part of my life training for this chance and I knew I needed every minute of it.

Fortunately, I was comfortable with myself as a gymnast. Mako had mapped out the course and I'd followed. I was lucky that he'd always been uncompromising. When he said dues were due, you paid them. He didn't waste a lot of time.

I was willing to do what the successful gymnast needed to be willing to do. And that meant I was willing to do what my coach told me to do. When Mako held me back from competing, I didn't compete. When he told me at age 16 not to join the national team yet, even though I had qualified, I didn't join the national team. Whatever he said, I did. There were times I would have preferred doing things a little differently, if *I* had been in charge, but I wasn't . . . and I didn't. We were a team. We had our roles and we stuck to them.

I certainly couldn't argue with where it took me—even if I did lose the Olympic all-around competition to Koji Gushiken by twenty-five thousandths of a point.

It remains the closest all-around battle in Olympics history. Gushiken, the 27-year-old three-time Olympian from Japan who was coming back from ankle and knee operations, and Vidmar, the 23-year-old Olympic rookie from Los Angeles, locked into a blow-for-blow on the final day that wasn't settled until I dismounted from my final event, the parallel bars, and hopped, oh, maybe two inches on my landing. I got a score of 9.9. A 9.95 would have given me the gold medal—by those same twenty-five thousandths of a point that I lost by.

It's funny. Finishing within twenty-five thousandths of the Olympic all-around title and, later, finishing seventh in floor exercise were as significant as anything I ever accomplished as a gymnast. In the all-around I was a fraction from the best in the world. I wound up finishing ahead of Li Ning, the pre-Olympic favorite from China, to name just one of those I expected to be looking up to in my home town, and I'd literally come within a hop-step of winning the whole thing. Mary Lou Retton became *Sports Illustrated*'s Sportswoman of the Year for doing it a day later . . . oh well.

And in floor exercise I'd always felt like a Sunday driver in the Indy 500. Like I didn't really belong. I really had no business even making the finals on floor—if I had any business being on the floor, period. I never had been blessed with strong legs—they didn't call me "Chicken Legs Vidmar" at the gym for no good reason—and as a result my tumbling was always, well, I guess you could say "under-powered." From where I started as a tumbler to where I finished—seventh in the world—was by far my biggest accomplishment as a gymnast. Nothing else came close. Personally I took more satisfaction in that seventh-place finish than anything.

But I certainly wasn't the first to discover that the world isn't all that interested in how far you've come or a lot of details as to why you didn't finish first. There was hardly any attention given to my seventh-place finish on the floor, and despite the thrilling finish in the all-around, the fact that I won the silver medal and not the gold—no matter how narrow the margin—quickly turned that story into yesterday's news. I finished in fourth place in rings, just a tenth of a point out of first place and one spot out of the medals, so that wasn't a big story either. Mitch Gaylord won three medals in the individual finals, a silver and two bronzes, all in the same day. One of the best medal hauls by a U.S. male gymnast in a century! And it was mostly a footnote to the gold medal he won with the team.

Mary Lou Retton, who would win the women's all-around title the next night by just five hundredths of a point over Ecaterina Szabo of Romania, became one of the biggest stories of the L.A. Games—and Szabo became an afterthought. The world is interested mainly in whose flag they're raising and whose anthem they're playing. The world loves first place. I love first place too (but I also like seventh).

Perfect, You Can Look It Up

As I've said, the easiest gymnastics event for me was the pommel horse. The pommel horse isn't temperamental like the rings can sometimes get. It doesn't talk back like the high bar. And to do it you don't have to have King Kong's legs. Sometimes it can actually be fun. For me, at least, it was fun. It was love at first flight.

So it was no surprise to me or anyone else when the horse was my strongest event in the Olympics.

The situation facing me was as exacting as it was mathematically simple. Li Ning of China was the leader in the clubhouse, as they say, and to catch him I had to score a nice, round, even number—a 10.

Somehow, just knowing I had to be perfect to tie for the gold medal had a calming effect on me. Certainly no one *expected* perfection, including myself. I decided I didn't have anything to lose and I still had plenty to gain. Plus, this was one of the final acts of the Games—and Peter Vidmar's competitive gymnastics career. No longer did I need to worry about pacing myself. I could go all out and if I collapsed, well, so what? I'd have the rest of my life to recover.

Besides, I'd spent better than half my life preparing for this one moment. This is why I didn't play on the high school baseball team. This is why I only surfed when my coach wasn't looking. This is why I went to bed early on Friday nights and tried to eat the right foods and never went to Yosemite with the Boy Scouts. This is why, for the better part of the previous dozen years, I'd worked myself to a fever pitch.

There are worse feelings than feeling due.

I have watched many athletic performances since those Olympic Games of 1984. I have watched, in particular, a lot of Olympic performances, both live and on television. And when I look at an athlete about to begin a competition that has an enormous consequence attached to it, because of my own experience I have a sense of awareness and an appreciation for the situation he or she is in. I always find myself hoping that they're prepared. It's when you're prepared that you have a chance, a real chance.

There's no substitute for it. It's when you've done the work, you've paid the price, and then some, and you know it, that you find this huge reservoir to dip into when it's finally time to show what you've got. The great champions, the ones whose examples are worth watching and memorizing, click into that tremendous confidence that comes from preparation. And more often than not, they come through.

Look around, and you can see it in all walks of life. From the pianist in concert to the car salesman who really knows his product. From plumbers to car mechanics to second basemen to ballerinas. From bus drivers to bank tellers to teachers to contestants on *Jeopardy*. People who have put in the preparation to the point that when the situation calls for a high level of expertise— for real virtuosity—they come through.

When I faced the pommel horse for the final competitive time on August 4, 1984, what I had going for me was my history and my preparation. The task in front of me was no great shock. This was what I had trained for. I didn't know if I *would* do it, but I did know I had been trained so I *could*.

I had one thought, and that was to go all out. That was Plan A. There was no Plan B. No easier routine to pull out of my bag of tricks in case I wasn't feeling great that day. Plan A called for all the risk, all the originality, and all the virtuosity I had left. Drain the reserves. Empty the accounts.

I'd practiced that one pommel horse routine over and over again, practiced it to the point where I never wanted to see it again.

If there had been another choice I might have taken it, because even if I did feel fairly calm, perfection is more than just a little bit to ask, and I could easily have decided that perfection was out of reach and so, to be safe, I would simply cut back to make sure I won the silver medal, or at least the bronze.

The only thing I knew for sure is that as soon as my toes overlapped or my legs came apart or I inhaled when I meant to exhale I would lose the gold medal. I had to be perfect, is all. So I did not ease into things. From the first double leg circle I was at full throttle.

Which was fine at the beginning because I had this huge surge of adrenaline kick in and I felt great!

But at about the two-thirds point of the routine the warning lights started to come on the dashboard. I had never gone this hard this fast. I could feel my body starting to tighten up. I felt like a 400-meter runner who's gone out too hard when he's coming into the final curve. That fluid feeling was beginning to leave my body. The lactic acid was setting in. Cramping couldn't be far behind.

The nagging fear at the end of the tunnel was my dismount—a back travel down the length of the horse, followed by that handstand dismount I'd invented by accident. Not a dismount to trifle with. It was the skill that could get me a 10, or get me burned.

So I thought to myself, *You're cramping up Peter, pull out of the hard dismount.* My reasoning was simple. If I substituted an ordinary dismount and finished with good form I could probably score high enough to get a medal, and I'd already done well enough that perhaps the judges wouldn't even notice.

Then I thought, *Nah, they'll notice. You can't have a trademark dismount and then not do it, even though there's no law against it, because the judges are going to say, 'Peter backed out,' and they'll deduct points.*

The debate I'm describing to you raged in my mind for the better part of, oh, about a second and a half.

I was flying through my routine and I didn't have time for any more deliberation. The jury wasn't out long. Verdict: *Peter . . . Do what you trained to do!*

That decision gave me new life. Suddenly I felt an extra surge of adrenaline and that was great because as I approached the dismount I realized I wasn't cramping up any more and I felt stronger than ever.

I performed the difficult backward travel across the horse and then I surged to the handstand and stuck the landing. Didn't hop an inch.

I found myself thinking *Great!* as I saluted the head judge for what would be my last time as a competitor. *That's as good as I can do. That's as good as I can expect. That had to be a 9.95!*

I still didn't want to hope for perfection. I didn't dare hope for a perfect score.

Then I looked up just as they flashed my score—a 10—and I had this incredible feeling shoot from my toes through the top of my head.

It's difficult to describe the emotions that were swirling around at that moment. I was standing in Pauley Pavilion at UCLA, my alma mater, in my home town of Los Angeles. All of my close friends and family were watching. My father, who beat polio before I was ever born, was there. My mother, who had escorted me to the Culver City Junior High girls' gym to meet Coach Mako Sakamoto and who always made sure I got to practice (and everywhere else) on time, was there. My wife, Donna, who was working at a camera position for a Bud Greenspan film production, was there. Coach Mako stood just a few feet away, his whole bearing reflecting the reality that we'd done together what we set out to do.

Eight miles away, the Culver City Junior High gym still stood too, dark on this night, the gymnastics equipment, as always, stowed against the wall or away in lockers, out of sight.

Twelve years to travel eight miles for a gold medal.

The fact that it took a 10 to get it only capped the story.

I was lucky. I was fortunate. I was blessed. I'll admit to all of that and more. And the biggest benefit of all, I've come to realize, wasn't winning the gold medals; it was the realization that 10's are possible. I was never an extraordinary athlete. In some ways I had considerable limitations. I was short. I had chicken legs. But I came to realize that pursuing 10's means capitalizing on what you have, not on what you don't have. That's what I learned in my Olympic odyssey.

I've seen firsthand what can happen when a strong foundation is joined by risk, originality and virtuosity. The truth is, not only can we all chase 10's; sometimes we can even catch them.

Part III

Do It

"The essential thing is not to have conquered, but to have fought well."

PIERRE DE COUBERTIN, FOUNDER OF THE MODERN OLYMPIC GAMES

"Let's play ball."

ROY HOBBS TO THE UMPIRE IN *THE NATURAL*

AFTER I "RETIRED" following the Olympics and began speaking to various groups about my experiences, I found it was easier for me to bring along the pommel horse. That way I could show them what I was trying to say. The way some people talk with their hands, I talk with my pommel horse.

Luckily, I wasn't a swimmer.

Over time, the horse has become a big part of "the act." To the point that I wouldn't feel right on a stage without it. Before each speech, no matter where it might be, I always find a local gymnastics club and arrange to borrow a pommel horse. I guess you could say I've turned myself into the world's foremost authority on the location of pommel horses. Name a city, and I can tell you where they keep their pommel horses.

At first, I thought it was just plain good luck, my transition from "competitive gymnast" to "talking gymnast." I remember having lunch with a friend not long after the Olympics when the subject of my "encore career" as a speaker came up, and I said that it had happened quite by chance.

But the more I thought about it, I realized that chance wasn't really as much of a factor as I might have originally thought. As with most things in life, there was much more involved than sheer happenstance. The more I looked at it, the more I realized that as I moved on beyond the Olympics I instinctively stuck to the course I'd learned as a gymnast: namely, the tried and true course of risk, originality, and virtuosity. New day, same stuff. What worked in gymnastics, can work beyond gymnastics.

That, in essence, is the message of this book.

R.O.V. works.

It's worked for me.

Twice.

In two careers.

Whatever our pursuits in life, if we'll take calculated risks, if we'll strive for originality, and if we'll perform with virtuosity, we'll put ourselves in the best position to realize our goals. That's my message. I've found a sound formula for success. I'm confident the results will please, and probably surprise, you—as they have me.

First Things First

Although it wasn't the primary objective, it was lucky for me that my Olympic training had such a strong carryover effect. I sure didn't train as a gymnast for twelve years to prepare myself for another career. Success in life wasn't the object. Success as a gymnast was. Remember that ad I answered in the *Santa Monica Evening Outlook*? It was for a program that would "develop future Olympic champions." That's what it said. And that's what it did. I sure couldn't sue Mako Sakamoto for breach of contract.

Only occasionally while I was training would I sneak a thought about what I might do after the Games were over—when I'd be over the hill at the ripe old age of 23. I got my degree at UCLA in economics, and in the back of my mind I assumed I'd become some kind of a "businessman." After the Olympics I thought I'd probably go on to get a graduate degree in business. I could foresee the day when I'd buy some suits and ties and leather-soled shoes and commute to a downtown L.A. office building, where I'd work for a brokerage house, perhaps, or maybe a large corporation. I was going to grow up.

A business career was appealing to me for a number of reasons, but it was all just a kind of fuzzy appeal because of the attention I needed to constantly put on gymnastics. I knew what was required to have a shot at being "a future Olympic champion" and I simply didn't have the luxury of daydreaming beyond that. If I ever did get very far off track, Mako was always there to bring me back.

In the months that led up to the Games, several guys on the team signed with agents and began laying the groundwork to capitalize on whatever post-Olympic opportunities might come up. Bart Conner already had a television contract. Mitch Gaylord's agent got him on the cover of *Esquire*. Knowing that this was going on, I approached Mako one day and asked him, "Do you think I should get an agent?"

From a man who once took his family on a car vacation from Los Angeles to Yellowstone and back *over the weekend* so he wouldn't miss Monday afternoon's practice, you can probably guess the response.

"What for?" he said.

"Well, it seems everyone else is doing it, I guess to get ready for endorsements and stuff after the Olympics," I said.

As he always did, Mako reeled my perspective back in, reminding me why the two of us had gotten together in the first place. "You know, Pete, if you win a gold medal at the Olympics I'll bet you could make a lot of money," he said, surprising me. "But don't let that be the reason for doing gymnastics. Let's just train. If you win it will happen. But don't prepare for that. Just train."

Don't get the steps out of order, in other words. You might trip. That's what he was telling me. In one way or another, he'd been telling me that since the first day I met him. First, set your goals; next, lay the foundation, and then build on it in an orderly way.

As it's turned out, the foundation for what I would do after the Olympics meant first winning those gold medals. I realize the medals are the main reason anyone has an interest in listening to what I have to say. Success opens doors. Success gives you a voice. If Lou Holtz were a sub-.500 coach at a community college, he wouldn't be in demand as a speaker, no matter how entertaining he is. If Tom Peters hadn't first written *In Search of Excellence*, he wouldn't have been one of the world's most sought-after corporate speakers.

But if that had been the reason I trained; if the impetus behind my quest for the gold was so I could then book dates on the speaker's circuit, then that would have changed the stakes. Not only would it have changed the pressure, but, with financial security and post-Olympic success added to the cause, it would have turned it into an entirely different kind of cause, weighed down by considerably more factors. Most important, I would have diluted the purity of my quest simply to try to do perfect gymnastics.

I didn't need that kind of baggage, or pressure, and if I didn't know it, Mako did. He knew that if I concentrated on the task at hand and I was able to lay a foundation that was built on Olympic success, the rest would all fall into place. First things first. I'd have plenty of time and opportunity to develop my next career; and the good part is I'd be able to use the discipline I'd already learned as a gymnast.

What I've discovered is that while the pursuits may change, the formula remains the same. As a gymnast, I first laid a foundation of coaching, support, learning the basics, and teamwork. I didn't rush it. I didn't compete before I was ready. I prepared first. Then, it was to that solid foundation that I added some risk, some originality, and some virtuosity.

Once I won the gold medals at the Olympics, I began laying another foundation in the same way as the old one. Call it force of habit or automatic pilot, but what I did after the Games was to continue to do what I had done as a gymnast.

They Pay You for This?

It took a while to get focused. As with a lot of gold medalists, I admit I was enticed by this new, if minor, stardom. Gymnastics tours, a television contract, perhaps, and maybe some endorsements. Hey, I'm from L.A., how about a movie? Speaking wasn't something I paid much attention to. It wasn't something that I did.

The first time I was asked to speak, I was surprised anyone would want to listen to what I had to say.

The Olympics were just beginning when I called my dad from the pay phone in the Olympic Village. He said his boss had just called, the chairman of the board of a large international company, and wondered if I'd be interested in speaking at their biannual chairman's meeting in a few weeks.

"They want *me* to speak?" I said.

"That's what they told me," he said.

"Where?" I asked.

"Bermuda," he said.

"I'll be there," I said. "Can I bring my wife?" I added, pushing my luck.

"Yes, she's invited . . . and they'll pay you."

"No way."

"Way!"

"I'll be there."

Then I wondered what the catch was or if maybe, just maybe, he might be putting me on, so I said, "Let me get this straight, Dad. Your company wants me to give a speech to them and it's in Bermuda and they'll fly me there and I can bring Donna and they're going to pay me?"

He reaffirmed all that.

"I'm in! . . . Hey Dad, what they want me to talk about?"

"I don't know, son," my father said dryly. "The Olympics, I guess."

So Donna and I went to Bermuda and that's when I gave a primitive version of the R.O.V. speech that has since become a big part of my post-Olympic motivation.

It Took a While

That first speech in Bermuda didn't set off any light bulbs in my head, that speaking to corporate America would, or could, be a new career. There was only so much demand for a medal-winner from Los Angeles, particularly since there had been quite a few Americans come out of those Games with positive Olympic tales to tell. For the most part I started to spin my wheels.

It was then, when I was scrambling, left as it were to myself, that I got back to my roots of risk and originality. That's when old instincts kicked in—and things started to happen.

I got on the phone and personally called a number of speakers' bureaus myself. I explained to the different booking agents what I did as a speaker. I told them I gave motivational talks, with pommel horse, that were based on my Olympic experiences and the pursuit of a perfect 10 and I was available to any size company or audience.

There was still plenty of patriotic Olympic fervor in America lingering from the success of the Los Angeles Games and I hoped to be able to particularly capitalize on those companies or groups that wanted to continue to affiliate with the Olympic movement. I made sure I contacted those companies that were already involved with the Olympics as sponsors or benefactors, and appealed to them in the context of future Olympics, not just what had gone on in the past. I was in what were, for me, uncharted waters, and if nothing else, I wanted to use some common sense.

I also instinctively knew I needed to take some risks.

As much as anything, I was riding a hunch, and there were absolutely no guarantees that I'd get any kind of return at all for my efforts. I didn't know if I'd even be able to cover my phone bill. And probably worse than the financial risks I was taking, I was wading into an area where I could easily get rejected. By 1984 the Olympic movement had been underway for the better part of a century and how many Olympic athletes, really, had gone this speaking route, let alone made a living at it? The answer is: Not many. Dr. Bob Richards, the American pole vault champion from the Olympics of 1952 and 1956, had become a motivational speaker and minister, and a few others had dabbled in motivational speaking, but it was a short list. If you looked at a short list of the top motivational speakers, it was dominated by successful businessmen, and some returned prisoners of war, along with a few successful coaches. There were no Olympic athletes, gymnastics or otherwise, to be found.

Any number of Olympians have turned their gold medals into box office success, of course—led by the swimmer Buster Crabbe, who won one gold medal in the 1932 Los Angeles Olympics and then made no less than 192 movies. Before Hollywood was through with him, he played Buck Rogers, Captain Gallant, Billy the Kid, Thunda the Jungle Man, Flash Gordon, and Tarzan (one of four Olympic medalists to play that part—curiously, despite all that vine swinging, none of them gymnasts). And still more gold medalists had gone on to become television commentators.

Other Olympians through the years have become corporate spokespersons or they've used their names to endorse any number of products. Indeed, the game of turning Olympic success into economic success is as old as the Games themselves. As William Oscar Johnson reports in *The Olympics, A History of the Games*, champions of the ancient games in Greece, after being sent home with a sacred wild olive wreath atop their heads, were set up for life. "Everyone knew well that there was more booty to come," Johnson writes. "Once the hero got home he was routinely given money and property. Streets were named for him, and the likes of Pindar or Euripides would sometimes toss off the odd ode in his honor."

I didn't expect to be given anything. Once again, I didn't do gymnastics for that. And I certainly didn't think anyone would be writing any odes about me or naming any streets after me, but I did think my success might open some doors, if I just knew where to find them. And just because motivational speaking was something of a road less traveled for Olympic athletes didn't mean it couldn't qualify.

So I risked some time, some effort, some money, and some pride, and made those initial "cold calls," not knowing where they might lead me.

I have to admit, I liked the feeling. I liked being out there on the mat again, if only figuratively, taking those risks. The old competitive instincts returned.

Practically everybody on the team was asked to give a speech or two right after the Games. And it's funny, we all wanted to wear suits. We didn't want to go as gymnasts. We wanted to go as successful businessmen—in the uniform of the people we were typically addressing. I remember Tim Daggett asking me, "Man, do they always ask you to perform too?" And I said, "Yeah. But I want to wear a coat and tie."

I wanted to look corporate. I wanted to act corporate. I wanted to grow up. We all did. We wanted to walk out in front of all these business people and tell them how gymnastics is done and how that relates to selling widgets, and then walk off to their applause. But everyone kept altering my plan to become this corporate icon by asking me to do my dog and pony show—you know, my skit, a gymnastics show, the pommel horse. They wanted me to wear my uniform and be a gymnast.

Finally, the light went on. I realized, Hey! I *am* a gymnast. This sells. People like this! This is what they want! And I can tell the demand has not gone down. To this day I can count on one hand the number of speeches I've given not wearing my U.S.A. uniform and performing on the pommel horse.

The nice part is that as I get further away from the Olympics I realize how lucky I've been to be able to combine my sport with my vocation. It gives me the double advantage of having a good reason to stay in shape and to stay involved in my sport. I'm still doing gymnastics. How lucky is that!

Applications

Beyond the workplace and beyond the professional world, R.O.V. can just as easily be applied to other areas in life. Interpersonal relationships on all levels can be enhanced with risk, originality, and virtuosity.

What marriage relationship couldn't benefit from a healthy dose of all three? What if a marriage were like a gymnastics meet and the goal of each participant (spouse) was to score a 10? Both spouses' routines (their performance in the relationship) would, by definition, be loaded with as much risk, originality, and virtuosity as possible. They'd want to practice overtime on their weaknesses, they'd want to anticipate the other person's needs, they'd do everything they could to not be boring and predictable, and they'd have great perseverance.

In other words, they'd act a lot like they did when they were dating.

In other family relationships the same principles apply. Just as it takes effort to win a gold medal, or a promotion at work, or a sales contest, or any number of worthwhile pursuits, it takes effort to establish and maintain satisfying interpersonal relationships. Looking at a marriage or a friendship, or any other intimate relationship, in the same context as looking at a quest for a gold medal can help define the purpose. Far from demeaning it, it gives it focus as well as value. I suspect that if many of us applied the same fervor, energy and commitment to our interpersonal relationships as we do to our careers, our athletic pursuits, or any of a number of other personal hobbies and interests, we would enjoy significant results. We would enjoy our relationships more *because* of the amount of energy, fervor and commitment expended.

Goal!

If we look closely at any successful accomplishment, we'll invariably find two key ingredients:

1. Definable goals.
2. Plenty of healthy motivation.

As overused as the concept is, never underestimate the importance of goals and motivation. It's one thing to just want to be better, but it's so much more effective when we want to be better for reasons that are clear and compelling.

If my Olympic goal hadn't been distinctly in place for me, I know I wouldn't have had the same motivation to spend all those hours in the gym. What I was trying to accomplish made it harder, but it also made it easier. Worthwhile goals—goals we really want—are invaluable. It doesn't matter what anyone else thinks of our goals, what matters is what we think of them. Maybe some people don't want to win gymnastics Olympic medals. Maybe some companies couldn't care less about the Malcolm Baldridge Award for Quality. But for those who do care, it works. And for others, there are other motivators. The key is to find out what works for you.

Individuals need goals. Companies need goals. We all need goals. They are what give us direction. They give us *reasons.*

Olympic history is full of accounts that not only illustrate the value of goal-setting, but the almost otherworldly lengths Olympians have gone to in quest of their goals. No Olympic champion illustrates that any better than swimmer Mark Spitz, who, at the Munich Games in 1972, became the first person in history to win seven gold medals in one Olympic Games.

But to see Spitz's feat in context you have to go back to the Pan-American Games in 1967. In that competition—held every four years among countries in the Western Hemisphere—Spitz won five gold medals. It was after he won his fifth gold medal that he predicted he would better that by one the next year at the Olympics in Mexico City.

But the quest for six in Mexico came up well short as Spitz won two gold medals, and both of those were in relay races. He didn't win a single individual race. In light of his expectations and his previous accomplishments, he was bitterly disappointed.

He refused to let go of his goal of six gold medals, however. For the next four years he put his head down, went back to work, and was determined that when another Olympics rolled around in 1972 he would finally fulfill his prediction. For good measure, he upped his gold medal goal to seven—one for each event he hoped to swim.

The defeats of '68 drove an even stronger work ethic in Mark Spitz, to the point that by those '72 Games in Munich he was, for all intents and purposes, swimming in a pool of his own. He won every gold medal he went after, seven of them in all, and set seven world records in the process—in the 100-meter freestyle, the 200-meter freestyle, the 100-meter butterfly, the 200-meter butterfly, the 100-meter freestyle relay, the 400-meter freestyle relay, and the medley relay. No one in any sport in Olympic history has ever won as many gold medals in a single Olympics.

Twenty-four years after Spitz's superlative show in Munich, another show-stopping Olympic performance, this one by sprinter Michael Johnson, provided yet another dramatic reminder of not just the importance of goals, but of using past disappointments to help fuel the drive toward those goals.

Johnson's goal at the 1996 Atlanta Olympic Games was to become the first person in Olympic history to win both the 200-meter and 400-meter races. Four years earlier, in Barcelona, he'd failed to medal in either race, despite being the favorite, when a bad case of food poisoning weakened him just before the start of the Olympics. Even more determined because of that disappointment, he trained for the Atlanta Games with an amazing focus. He left practically nothing to chance—including what he ate. Barcelona had taught him a lesson. Take nothing for granted. In advance of Atlanta, Michael Johnson took control of everything even remotely within his grasp. He even personally asked the International Olympic Committee to change its racing schedule to better accommodate his 200–400 quest, and his request was granted.

The result, of course, was historic. He first set an Olympic record in winning the 400 and then, 72 hours later, he set a world record in the 200, running three-tenths of a second faster than anyone in history at that distance.

I like the Mark Spitz and Michael Johnson stories because not only do they point out the value of setting goals, but, even more important, they point out that merely setting a goal isn't enough. Focus, hard work—and, yes, good timing—need to come before the accomplishment. (Goals have to be realistic, of course, but certainly in Spitz's case, after winning five gold medals at the Pan Am Games, setting a goal to do even better than that at the Olympics couldn't be viewed as unrealistic.) We can set all the goals we like, but unless we're willing to bear down and do what it takes to get there, we won't get very far in realizing them.

I've had plenty of experiences to vouch for that personally. I made my first national gymnastics team at the age of 16, when I placed thirteenth at the finals held at UCLA. Then my coach took me off the team, reasoning that I'd be better off spending the next year working out in the gym than being thrown into the heart of international competition I wasn't really ready for.

The problem was, I didn't use that year as effectively as I could have. I got cocky and sometimes just went through the paces in practice. I told myself I was working as hard as I could, but I really wasn't. I'd already made the national team and I took a lot of stock in that. I was resting on that "laurel" even if I didn't realize it. My ultimate goal as a gymnast—to become a world champion—had not changed, but I'd shifted into cruise control. I wasn't bearing down like I had in the past. I guess in a way I thought I'd already made it.

Then, a year later, when the nationals rolled around again, I showed up for my encore performance, my triumphant re-entry to the national scene . . . and I finished thirteenth. Again. I hadn't improved even one place.

That got my attention. Mako's too! I'd essentially been treading water for a year—not unlike what Mark Spitz had done in between winning those five gold medals in the Pan-Am Games and waiting to win six more.

The morning after my second nationals I was back in the gym with a different attitude. My goals were all still firmly planted ahead of me, but I realized that in the past twelve months I hadn't gained any ground. I got busy after that. I would say that in the next three months I improved more as a gymnast than anytime in my development. Not long after that I placed sixth at the final trials for the World Championships. The six-man U.S. team went to the World Championships and won this country's first world championship team medal in eighty years. I'd improved seven spots in three months, then went on to be a medallist at the World Championships. Sometimes you need a wake-up call.

Whatever Works

One of my all-time favorite Olympic "goal" stories involves a rower named Jack Kelly. Jack Kelly was a tough kid from Philadelphia who trained on the Schuylkill River and dreamed of one day rowing in the famed Diamond Sculls race at the Royal Henley Regatta on the Thames River in England. In rowing, the Royal Henley is the Super Bowl and World Series rolled into one, and every day when he'd work out on the Schuylkill that's what fueled Jack Kelly's training. One day he would go to Henley-on-Thames and row against the very best.

But this was just after the turn of the century and, like a lot of things back then, rowing had a rather ruthless caste system. The rules at the Thames race said you weren't eligible to compete if you worked with your hands (kind of odd when you think about what a rower does, but that's the way it was. It tended to keep the riffraff out and the good old boys from Oxford and Cambridge in). Well, Jack Kelly had been a bricklayer as a boy and so they sent back his application for the 1920 competition. It was stamped "unacceptable."

He had no recourse but to accept his fate—and point for a competition where he might have a shot at the rowers he wouldn't get to face in London. The upcoming Olympic Games in Antwerp, Belgium, filled that bill nicely. Already a two-time national champion in single sculls, Kelly easily made the 1920 United States Olympic team and soon set sail with the United States team for Belgium. There, he and an Englishman heavily favored to win the gold medal, Jack Beresford, engaged in a furious sprint along the 2,000 meters of the single sculls final course. Beresford, as fate would have it, was fresh from winning the title at that year's Diamond Sculls race at Henley. That proved to be more than enough motivation for Kelly, who surged just ahead of the British boat at the finish line, winning by one second. History notes that both men were so tired afterward they could not sit up to shake hands.

Later, while standing on the victory podium, Kelly took off his kelly green hat and waved it to the crowd—and then, in a kind of coup de grace of defiance, sent it to King George of England.

There's also an interesting footnote to this story. More than a quarter of a century later, in 1947, Jack Kelly's son, Jack Jr., sent his application to row at the Diamond Sculls at Henley. He was accepted—and, while wearing a kelly green hat, he won.

Later, Jack Kelly, Jr. became the president of the United States Olympic Committee. You may also have heard of another of Jack Kelly's children, Grace. She made a name for herself as well, first as a popular Hollywood actress and then as the Queen of Monaco.

Positive Motivation

In my travels as a speaker, I've noticed that the successful companies and corporations I've become acquainted with, as well as the successful individuals, seem to not only understand the need for motivation but the need to structure that motivation. They realize that motivation is too important to be left to chance.

A few years ago, in my work with the Governor's Council on Physical Fitness and Sport in California, I've had a chance to associate with Rear Admiral Ray Smith (now retired) of the United States Navy. Admiral Smith was a commander at the Naval Special Warfare Command on Coronado Island in San Diego, where the Navy trains its elite of the elite, the Navy SEALS. These soldiers who make the SEALS are among the fittest human beings on planet earth. Their training is rigorous and sometimes around the clock. During the SEALS' "hell week" they only let them sleep four hours—for the entire week.

One thing the SEALS are proud of is their obstacle course, where they hold periodic races that help them monitor their physical fitness. I casually told Admiral Smith I'd like to give "The O-course" a try. That was my first mistake.

They let me try the course one afternoon after our physical fitness council had held its morning meetings near the base. I went in the middle of a group of SEALS, five in front of me, five in back, and we went off at twenty-second intervals. They issued me the standard combat wear, complete with combat boots (much lighter than I expected), and I was off.

The course began with a hand-walk across parallel bars—no sweat there—but that was just the introduction. Then came logs, a twelve-foot wall to scale, a twenty-foot rope to climb, a rope ladder that was at least fifty feet off the ground, a free-floating log that rolls if you're off balance, more logs, a twenty-foot dive under barbed wire, more ropes, a rope bridge they call the Burma Bridge, a structure I call the tower of death (a four-floor building with no stairs), another rope, another log, a rock-climbing wall, and, finally, the unaptly named finish line. As soon as you cross it you're still not finished—until you drop and give them twenty pushups.

If you can't do the course in fifteen minutes they won't keep you in the SEALS. The first time I did it in eight minutes and thirty seconds. The world record is around five minutes.

Negotiating that course was one of the hardest physical things I've ever done. I went aneorobic about a third of the way through and stayed there until I'd somehow finished those pushups. I was totally exhausted. But the interesting part was this: Not long after I recovered I wanted to do it again. Maybe not right then, but soon. I knew where I thought I could make up time. I wanted another shot at it, to see if I could do better. (Later I was able to drop it down to 7 minutes and change, no better). In a similar manner, I'm sure that obstacle course works as an effective motivator for the troops enrolled in the SEALS program.

Focus

A key ingredient in the area of goals and motivation is having the proper focus. Another person I've become associated with while serving on the President's Council on Physical Fitness & Sport is Arnold Schwarzenegger. His focus is as sharp as anyone's I've ever seen. John Naber, the gold medal-winning swimmer, likes to tell the story of sitting around a table in the early '80's with a bunch of athletes, many of whom were at or near the ends of their competitive careers. Someone posed the question as to where they all imagined they'd be ten years later.

They went from person to person around the table. Many of the forecasts were ordinary and forgettable, but one that wasn't was the prediction from the muscle-bound guy from Austria.

Speaking English with a thick accent, the body-builder, who had just finished shooting *Conan the Barbarian*, brashly announced, "In ten years I'm going to be one of the biggest movie stars in the world. I'll be making over a million dollars a picture."

Here was a person who had spent most of his life in a gym lifting weights. He'd made one movie, which met with mixed reviews, and, at that, it was a part that primarily showed off his muscles. He had a thick accent and a name nobody could spell. And he was going to be an American film star?

He could have taken bets then and there, and *really* set himself up.

Universal Appeal

Go ahead, name a significant human achievement, and you'll find the ingredients of risk, originality, and virtuosity involved.

How about Christopher Columbus? He risked falling off the edge of the earth so he could pursue an original theory, considered absurd at the time, that the world was round. He felt he could reach Asia by sailing *west*. He needed plenty of virtuosity both as a diplomat—when he needed to win funding from the Spanish queen, Isabella—and as a sailor and captain to pursue, and reach, his goal.

And then, an interesting thing happened on the way to India . . .

Risk, originality, and virtuosity all played a big part in getting him to the new world. (Although, as is sometimes the case with originality, Columbus never fully realized just where he'd gotten. Till the day he died, some fourteen years following his famous voyage of 1492, he believed he'd actually reached the eastern shores of Asia.)

How about Thomas Edison? He invented the incandescent light bulb, which more than a century later seems significant enough. But that's only the part we see. Before he could even get around to inventing the light bulb, Edison had to deal with a cumbersome electricity system already in place in the mid-1800's that used generators called dynamos and lamps called arc lights. In other words, in order for his incandescent bulbs to have a chance to even have a *use*, he first had to invent an entire new electrical *system*. He had to *rewire the country*.

Just the idea of such a job caused all other inventors to turn away.

Only Edison was undaunted. He attacked the problems that seemed prohibitive to everyone else and solved them anyway. As a consequence of that kind of determination, Thomas Edison ushered in the Age of Electricity. We pay tribute to him every time we turn on a light switch.

Thomas Edison—who once said "Genius is one percent inspiration and ninety nine percent perspiration"—was willing to take the risks necessary to develop a completely new, completely untested, system of electricity. One he was convinced would be infinitely more practical, and less expensive, than the one already in place. Of further testament to his originality and virtuosity are the 1,093 patents registered to his name throughout his life (including those for the phonograph, the movie projector, the mimeograph machine, and talking movies). No one in history has registered more patents. The life of Thomas Edison can be inspiring to anyone looking for an example of one who was willing to experiment and think out his own solutions.

By the time of his death in 1931, when he was 84, Edison had successfully become a legend in his own time. It was suggested that a fitting tribute at his funeral would be to turn off the electric current throughout the nation for sixty seconds. But so widespread was the extent of Thomas Edison's "wiring" that the idea had to be scrapped. It would have brought the country to a standstill.

How about the Wright Brothers?

Wilbur and Orville Wright will forever be remembered as the pioneers of flight after Orville piloted their crude motorized airplane one hundred and twenty feet through the air during a twelve-second flight at Kitty Hawk, North Carolina, on Dec. 17, 1903. The risks the brothers took are obvious. To that point in the history of mankind, everything that went up, came down— usually in a hurry. The brothers were willing to risk life and limb in their effort to go airborne.

Their achievement came during a heated turn-of-the-century competition being waged by aeronautical inventors around the world. Following the invention of the internal combustion automobile in the late 1800's, there was considerable enthusiasm to extend motorized transportation to the air. In advance of their upcoming Expo, the promoters of the 1904 World's Fair in St. Louis offered a $100,000 prize to the first person or persons to successfully fly. The United States government also offered grants. Great inventors ranging from Thomas Edison to Alexander Graham Bell looked into the possibilities of air travel.

But no one got off the ground. The more they tried, the harder they crashed. The problem, as it turned out, was that the accepted "principles" of flying were inaccurate. The printed data that pertained to wing angles and air pressure was all wrong. The information everyone was basing their experiments on was completely inaccurate—and no one realized it.

Like Columbus and so many other revolutionary thinkers, the Wright Brothers dared to contradict, rather than embrace, conventional wisdom. They went back to square one and conducted their own experiments on wing angles and air pressure, after which they changed the data on their charts. As a result of their originality, they soon turned the race for space into a one-team competition. When they stopped copying everyone else and stopped relying on what had been accepted in the past, they were able to finally go up where no man had gone before.

On that windy day in North Carolina, when Orville's 12-second flight was followed by a 59-second, 852-foot flight by Wilbur, they scored their own 10.

Put It to the Test

Observing, analyzing, and dissecting the paths taken to success by others can be an effective way for us to recognize the virtues of risk, originality and virtuosity. It can be a great help as we plot our own courses of action, our own game plans.

Look at someone you admire, someone who has accomplished something truly worthwhile. It doesn't have to be Columbus or Thomas Edison or the Wright Brothers. It doesn't have to involve great sums of money or inventions that have changed the world. It can be a close friend, a co-worker, a competitor. It can be someone famous or someone practically anonymous. It can even be you. The only requirement is that this person has enjoyed what, in your view, is a satisfying accomplishment. Something that has improved their life and brought them peace, contentment and satisfaction.

Now analyze what got them there. Look at the steps they took, the work they did, the things that were effective. Did they operate first from a stable foundation that included strong support from tutors, parents, teammates, family and others? Did this foundation create an atmosphere that made confidence and progress possible? With that in place, what evidence are there are of risks? Of originality? Of virtuosity?

Consider these extremes: Mother Teresa and the Girl Scout who lives in your neighborhood and every year sells you Girl Scout cookies. I consider both to be success stories. One is universally acclaimed for her selflessness and resounding success. The other is acclaimed for the same things, but only on your street.

Mother Teresa, of course, was the Catholic nun who organized the Missionaries of Charity in Calcutta, India, in 1950. Through unselfish service she developed an organization dedicated to helping the poor and the dying. Today that organization offers compassionate service in nearly one hundred countries on five continents around the world. In 1979, at the age of 69, Mother Teresa was presented the Nobel Peace Prize.

Hers is a story full of good examples of the effective use of risk, originality and virtuosity. Mother Teresa risked much. At the age of 36, when she made the decision to head out on her own, she was well established as a successful school teacher at her convent's school in Calcutta. Almost literally, she plunged into the poor and the dying in one of the poorest countries on earth. She risked physical disease and mental torment in her quest to establish something completely unique (original) from anything else her church offered. In the process, not only did she become a virtuoso at compassion, but her name has become a synonym for charity.

The Girl Scout in your neighborhood has a similar story, although not as noble and on a smaller scale. She is an ace at selling Girl Scout cookies. She sells more Girl Scout cookies every year by herself than entire Girl Scout *troops*. Every year she's the one who wins the trip to Disneyland or wherever they're taking the top sellers that year. Her secret is simple: She tells her customers that the cookies can be frozen. And not only that. They're better frozen. Especially the mint ones, which tend to be the most popular.

She has people who buy a year's worth of the mint cookies! (That would be me.)

So how does her experience fit with R.O.V.? Well, there are the usual risks that come with sales. Fear of rejection, fear of failure, fear or offending others. As for originality, her tip about freezing the cookies has made a big difference in her sales. And in the department of Virtuosity, the longer she's worked at it, the better she's become.

Fighting the Good Fight

Speaking of Mother Teresa, consider another legendary peacemaker, Mahatma Gandhi.

The entirety of Gandhi's homespun life was dedicated to taking risks, to original ideas, and to developing virtuosity. Few world leaders in history have exhibited such consistency and loyalty to their cause.

Almost everything Gandhi was involved in was a powderkeg of human emotion. If he wasn't working to free India from British rule he was trying to promote religious harmony among the Hindus and Muslims. He spent his life devoted to the two subjects we're all warned to stay away from: religion and politics.

His risks were enormous. So enormous that he eventually paid for them with his life (he was assassinated by a Hindu fanatic). And for years before that, his life was in constant danger.

But amid all this conflict Gandhi found success and made headway where others failed because of his refusal to answer violence with more violence. His philosophy of *satyagraha* (literally, "steadfastness in truth") was that when someone hit you, you did not hit back. That didn't mean that you forsook your principles, it just meant that you did not answer back physically.

Gandhi protested peacefully and led others in peaceful protest all his life, but always without aggression. The British constantly put him in jail, and he constantly went on hunger strikes and got out. In the end, that produced better results than all the bullets in all the guns in India.

The kind of independent thinking demonstrated by a Mahatma Gandhi is clearly capable of producing dramatic results. We don't *have* to do it the way it's always been done. There's no law that says we can't chart our own course. No matter what field we're in. No matter what we're trying to accomplish.

There is an auto mechanic who personifies this. His name is Kurt Kimball and he works on high-end German-made cars, primarily BMW and Mercedes-Benz. Kurt was living in Los Angeles and running his own mechanic business several years ago when he took a weekend trip to the Santa Barbara area ninety miles to the north of L.A. As he was driving through Montecito, the town that borders Santa Barbara and is one of the wealthiest areas in the country—home to numerous movie stars and Hollywood producers—he came to a four-way stop. As he waited for his turn to go he noticed that every car around him was either a BMW or a Mercedes-Benz.

Well, you probably saw this coming, but a light went on in Kurt's head. Why not relocate to the place where a Mercedes is called a "Montecito Chevrolet?"

Within a couple of weeks he took the risk, made the move, and opened "Granny's Garage" of Santa Barbara.

His instincts, as it turned out, were right. There was a big demand for BMW and Mercedes mechanics in the Santa Barbara area. Not that there wasn't plenty of competition. One of the first things that became obvious to Kurt was that the car owners in Santa Barbara tended to do a lot of shopping around. If they didn't like the service or the price they got at one garage, they'd go to another. The mechanic business can be, in general, a fickle business, but even more so, it seemed, in Santa Barbara.

To counter that problem, Kurt Kimball decided it would be company policy at Granny's Garage that no one would ever—EVER—argue with a customer. If a customer wanted a lower price, company policy was to respond with, "All right, tell me what you think is fair," and if a customer ever returned with a complaint about the work done on his or her car, the problem would be cleared up then and there, no charge.

The result: more satisfied customers than any garage has a right to expect. And Kurt Kimball and his family are living happily next to those customers in the heart of Montecito.

We could go on and on with success stories of "real originals" and their effective employment of risk, originality and virtuosity. The examples are practically limitless.

Judging and Success—They Don't Always Go Hand in Hand

It's important to always keep in mind that success can often be very difficult to measure, and there is danger in assessing triumph or failure by external means.

We're talking about judging—and as any gymnast will tell you, judging is a very tricky subject.

Basically, there are two kinds of judgments in life. Objective and subjective.

Objective is defined in the dictionary as *"Without bias or prejudice; detached, impersonal . . . independent of the mind; real; actual."*

Subjective is defined as *"Of or resulting from the feelings or tem-*

perament of the subject; not objective; personal . . . not just rigidly tran-scribing or reflecting reality."

A baseball umpire defines the difference every time he works behind the plate.

When the umpire calls a pitch a strike because the batter swung and missed, that's an *objective* call.

When the umpire calls a pitch a strike when the batter does not swing, that's a *subjective* call.

Objective is black-and-white, straightforward, without argument. Subjective—and this is the kind of judging we have to be wary of—isn't.

Most judging in life is subjective.

I have to admit, there were times when I wished I were competing in a sport where the final score didn't depend so much on subjective judging. I'd be envious when I'd watch sports like basketball, football and baseball—where the outcomes were decided on the scoreboard and you didn't have to bow to the judges when you were finished. I'd watch track meets, where every winner was decided by a tape measure or electronic timing, and think, Now *that* would be nice.

But the truth is, no sport, no quest, is completely without subjective judging. A football game is still subject to officials, who are constantly making "judgment" calls about holding and pass interference and so on. Even in boxing, the most basic of competition, most results are decided *after* the two guys in the ring get through pounding on each other. Sometimes the best fights are over the judge's scorecards.

Almost all competitions have some element of human discretion. A basketball game is still subject to officials, who are also constantly making "judgment" calls.

Olympic annals, of course, are full of judging controversies. The stories from figure skating alone could fill volumes. The French judge at the Salt Lake City Winter Olympics will never be forgotten. The same goes for gymnastics. Gymnastics history buffs still recall with vivid detail the 1966 world championships held in Dortmund, Germany. A member of the American women's team named Doris Fuchs-Brause was generally regarded as the best in the world on the uneven parallel bars. In the competition she did a routine that stopped everyone in their tracks. She just mesmerized the crowd. But not, as it turned out, the judges. When her score came up it was in the mid-9's, a good score but well behind the leaders. Even the pro German crowd was outraged. They booed for one hour and twenty minutes!

I remember attending the World University Games in Bucharest, Romania, in 1981 and watching the Romanian men's team, which had never before won a major international meet, win the gold medal because more than half of the judges were from Romania. I had just won the high bar championship at the U.S. nationals, where I scored a 9.8, and I did an even better routine at Bucharest. I mean, I nailed every single solitary skill and I just drilled my dismount. I turned and looked at the judges as if to say, "Take that!" And the judges looked at me as if to say, "Take that!" They gave me a 9.5. After that, I just wanted to go home.

The most spirited "judge-dueling" I ever personally witnessed was the next year, in 1982, at a special dual USA-USSR meet at the University of Florida gym in Gainesville, Fla. The first performer for the U.S. team was Phil Cahoy, a 1980 Olympian, who hit his floor routine fairly well. Then the scores flashed up. A 9.2 from one Russian judge, a 9.3 from another Russian judge. On the other end of the scale he got a 9.7 from one of the American judges and a 9.8 from another American judge. We all looked at each other and thought, this is going to be a war. Not between the gymnasts, between the judges. We were right, of course. All meet long, the disparities were so blatant. When you've got one judge saying a routine is a 9.2 and another saying it's a 9.8, that's huge. If they were watching a basketball game, that's like one saying he made the basket and the next one saying no, he missed the basket.

I could go on and on with stories about judging, but the point is . . . so what? Life isn't always going to be fair. Subjective judging isn't always going to be right. Not in gymnastics, not in anything.

We're constantly "subject" to the judgments of our bosses, our coaches, our teachers, our parents, our children, our spouses. And we're constantly making subjective judgments ourselves—about our own performances and about others as well. Sometimes the judging is fair and just. Sometimes it isn't.

We live in a subjective world.

That extends beyond the gym, of course. Worrying about anything that goes beyond the borders of our own control and power is an exercise in futility, a free ticket to frustration.

Real 10's

The point is, it's not healthy to worry unduly about outside judging. There are too many variables, too many mitigating circumstances, too many moving parts, for any scoreboard to be even close to infallible. People who "give their all" don't always finish in first place.

Most of the time, life just isn't like the movies. If it were, my best friend, Tim Daggett, would have had the chance to compete again at the Olympic Games in Barcelona in 1988. Tim and Scott Johnson were the only members from our '84 team who decided to try for another Olympics. Most of the rest of us had moved on to find our fortunes in the world, but not Tim. He was going to do it again.

He was right on course, too, until about eight months before the 1988 Games when he severely fractured his leg in an accident. Initially, his condition was so serious the doctors knew amputating his leg was a possibility. For weeks he could no nothing but lie in bed.

Tim managed to hang onto his leg, and after a long, difficult surgery he plunged into his rehabilitation. He did everything the physical therapists told him to do and more. Improbably, seven months after surgery, he managed to enter the Olympic Trials. I'd venture to say that no one at those Trials worked harder to get there, or wanted to make the Olympic team more, than Tim Daggett. Here was a guy who'd been the heart and soul of the L.A. Games and now he's back at the Trials, competing against younger gymnasts for one of six spots up for grabs for Barcelona. To add to the drama, he was coming off a nearly catastrophic injury.

Midway through the competition, the made-for-TV movie was progressing nicely. Tim was among the leaders, in good position to make the team. But reality set in when he realized an optional floor routine was just going to be too much to ask of his not-quite-healed leg. When he started his floor exercise routine he collapsed on a tumble and could not continue. The leg just wouldn't hold up.

Since Tim didn't wind up competing in Barcelona, it would be easy to say he "lost," and I suppose he did in strictly conventional terms. And yet, what he accomplished, given where he started and what he had to overcome, was nothing short of a resounding triumph. The real shame about Tim Daggett's quest for encore gold would have been if he had somehow considered himself a failure. He chose not to do that, and instead used that experience to help him become one of America's top gymnastics coaches. Besides being a commentator for NBC, Tim now runs a successful gym in his hometown of West Springfield, Massachusetts.

He couldn't have done that if he had left those '88 Trials and given himself a "1," instead of the "10" he deserved. If he'd given himself a "1" he'd probably still be sitting on a rock right now, staring out at the ocean, wondering *Why him?* Instead, he's developing some of the best gymnasts in the country.

Ultimately, the responsibility for judging rests with ourselves. We're the only ones who know all the whys, wherefores, circumstances, and obstacles. We know the effort we've applied. We know when we've done our best—and we know when we haven't. If we'll honestly judge ourselves, life might not become fair, but we'll be fair to ourselves.

Critical acceptance by the world at large relies so much on being in the right place at the right time. Good fortune is as important as good moves.

If at First You Do Succeed

The author John Grisham is another good example of this quality of trusting in your own judgment and not worrying about critical acclaim. Chances are, you've read a John Grisham novel. His books have sold in excess of sixty million copies and counting. But he wasn't always so well-known.

After three years of writing, he'd completed his first novel, *A Time to Kill*. That was in 1987. That manuscript was then rejected by no less than twenty-six publishers before it was finally released in June of 1988 by Wyndham Press, a small publishing house. Total sales were five thousand copies. Hardly the kind of achievement that, by itself, would prompt you to hurry back to your word processor and crank out another book.

But Grisham didn't judge himself according to how many books he sold. He wrote because he liked to write. Even before *A Time to Kill* was published, he'd started work on another book.

That second novel, *The Firm*, was first bought by Paramount for movie rights and then picked up by a major New York publishing house, Doubleday. Before long you couldn't walk through an airport lobby without seeing people reading their copy. *The Firm* jumped to the No. 1 spot on the *New York Times* bestseller list and stayed there for forty-six weeks. It was the best-selling novel of 1991. John Grisham, who had been writing novels for seven years, was just another overnight sensation.

Naturally, his New York publisher wanted to know if he would write another book.

He told them he already had.

A Time to Kill was re-published by Doubleday's paperback subsidiary, Dell. This time it sold over five million copies. The same book that had initially been met by yawns, that sold just five thousand books, vaulted onto the *New York Times* No. 1 position, just like *The Firm*—and the film rights to *A Time to Kill* were sold to Hollywood for six million dollars.

If John Grisham had applied only the "scoreboard" of book sales and public acceptance to his original effort, he might have stopped writing books altogether. As it is he has continued to write his legal thrillers, and all have met with resounding public success.

Our Own Judges

Then there are those things we do in life—and I believe they are the majority—that just aren't measureable by statistics or medals or money in the bank. If everything needs to have a score or result attached to it in order for it to have value and validity, then that eliminates some of the most significant human endeavors and interactions.

For instance, when I was growing up I had what I considered a perfect Little League baseball coach. Nobody gave him an award for it. His name was Pete Shepherd and he was a former minor leaguer. He had a real knack for knowing how to handle kids.

Pete used to give a game ball to one player after every game we played. I never qualified for the game ball. Until. . . . I'll never forget April 14, 1971. I played second base that day and I made nine outs. I was no phenom as a baseball player. In practice the week before I'd tripped over the bag covering first base and missed the ball completely. But on this day I fielded every ball that came to me cleanly. We were standing around the dugout at the end of the game, Pete was telling us about our next game and who was bringing the refreshments and then he turned to me and said, "Peter," and he threw me the game ball. If it was a movie it would be one of those scenes where it would take about four minutes for the ball to travel from his hand to my glove. For me, it was a great moment. He didn't make a big deal out of it, but he was the kind of coach who built you up and made you feel like you were worth something.

Many years later, when I was at Disneyland with President George Bush for an event called Olympic Sendoff Day, a man approached me. He stuck out his hand and said, "You probably don't remember me . . . ," and I said, "The heck I don't. You're the greatest Little League coach of all time! You're Pete Shepherd." I floored him.

Balancing Act

For most of us, especially as we get older and acquire more responsibility, real success is *not* being a world champion.

Through personal experience, I know what it takes to try to be the best in the world. And no matter what it is, it's going to be largely a selfish endeavor. When I was training to be "an Olympic champion" that took precedence over just about everything except breathing. To some extent, I was self-centered, self-consumed. My brothers and sisters gave me a nickname: "The Franchise." As in "Don't hurt 'The Franchise.'"

To be focused on one thing was fine when all I essentially had to worry about was me. I could work out six hours every day. I could follow my Olympic goal single-mindedly.

But if I did that now it would be at the expense of a lot of some other, more important things. I have a wife and five children I'd end up neglecting. I have a mortgage to pay. I have other obligations. I have a job. I have many volunteer obligations. All of these things are important to me and they all require portions of my time and attention. And the only way I can be responsible to them all is to have balance in my life. I have to balance my time. I have to balance my attention. I have to balance my goals.

So it's not going to be easy for me to be a world champion in anything. Yes, I'd like to be in the same physical condition as when I was competing. I took a lot of pride in that. I miss those days. I really do. But I can't afford six-hour daily workouts any more. I'd like to be the most successful speaker in the world too. I'd like to set records. Who wouldn't? But what would be the price? To do that, I'd have to work every week of the year. I'd have to devote the vast majority of my time to my business. And where would that leave my family? Where would that leave the relationships I have, and would like to continue to have? Where would that leave my charity work or my work with my church?

Sometimes I think it's harder to show restraint than to show dogged pursuit. It's so easy to get carried away in the quest to reach the top. We see that happen all the time. It's human nature to want to be the best. But at what cost?

Not long ago my father, long since retired, talked on this subject when he reflected on his career as a businessman. He looked back at the numerous relationships he'd developed with customers and co-workers all around the world, from Australia to Tokyo to his home base in Los Angeles. He told me that he once considered those relationships as important as anything in his life. When he was active in his career, they mattered a great deal. But after he retired, they lost that importance. They were still good friendships, but the mutual objectives and common work goals they had been based on were gone—and hence, so was a lot of the value in those relationships. Without that common ground, the need for them diminished. They weren't as important any more.

What *did* have enduring importance, he realized, were his family relationships. "Had I sacrificed my family for my business career, I'd have had nothing when it was over," he told me.

It's easy to fall into the trap of putting things on hold, of sacrificing everything to try to be the best. But is it worth it? In the long run?

There was a time in my life when I could afford to try to be the best. But that time has passed. There are some things I can't be now, because of the expense involved.

In all of it, I have to accept my roles and my limitations. I don't have the time to be everything I'd like to be—none of us does.

Time—and Time Out

For each of us, the demands on our time can be tremendous, but we all are allotted the same twenty-four hours per day. If we don't learn to balance our time and our energies, we will allow some things to be neglected and our frustration, as a result of that, will only mount.

Accepting those limitations of time is important. I try to separate my work from my play for that very reason. I know I could work all the time, we all could, but I don't want to do that. Since I'm basically in business for myself, whenever I take weeks off for family vacations, for instance, it is always going to be at the expense of potential earnings. I remember going on a mountain biking trip with my wife after turning down some very lucrative speaking engagements that would have required that I cancel the trip. At the first of the week I was thinking, "Man, this is one expensive bike ride," but by the end of the week I wasn't thinking that way at all. I was thinking I'd like to figure out a way to extend the trip. We had a great time and made a lot of memories.

I think it's important to make decisions based on looking back. I try to think, "OK, twenty years from now, how will I look at this decision?" That's why I try to make decisions to go on vacations and spend time with my family. In twenty years I don't think I'll be thinking, gee, I wish I'd given that speech instead.

Still Works

Maintaining balance in our lives doesn't eliminate the need for R.O.V., it makes it all the more important. All "balance" means is that we have more areas in which to incorporate risk, originality, and virtuosity. The same principles apply whether it's trying to be an Olympic gold medalist or a scoutmaster.

My life is hardly atypical now. It might have once been, when I was focusing my energy and attention to one thing: gymnastics. But now that I have moved into the "real world," with a family and a variety of responsibilities, I know I'm in a cast of millions. Virtually everyone I know in my age group has similar daily challenges and time restraints. I want to be a good husband, father, son, and friend. I want to be successful at my work. I want to make contributions to the various charity groups and organizations (such as USA Gymnastics, where I serve on the board of directors) that I am a part of. I want to keep active in my church. I want to stay in decent physical condition. I want to still have time to mountain bike and surf and just play around. And I want to leave enough time to socialize.

All those areas are as important to me. When they are put down on paper, the list is kind of overwhelming. Especially when you dissect it even further and realize that each area in and of itself requires considerable time, attention and energy. Donna and I have five children, for example, and when we say we want to be good parents, that can't be just a general statement. That means we want to be good parents to *each* of our five children. Each has to be taken individually. No two are exactly alike.

That's just one area of life—raising children—and it alone involves all kinds of intricate parts and challenges, as well as time and attention. The same concerns and issues apply for volunteer work, social activities, etc. These things are all important to me. They all have value. The challenge for me is to make sure I give them as much support as I'm capable of and do them for the right reasons. What usually works, I've found, is to find a specific area I can get excited about, and concentrate my efforts in that direction.

There are many more examples that could be cited, examples as varied as our interests and our goals. There is no limit to the areas of our lives that can be enhanced by a transfusion of R.O.V. In everything we do, and I do mean everything, if we'll add the dimensions of risk, originality and virtuosity they can enable us to reach higher, stretch farther, accomplish more, and enjoy the process more fully. In those areas where we're already doing all the requirements; where we've gone through all the paces and paid the price and established a solid level of adequacy; where all our support groups are in place and we've built as strong a foundation as possible; where we've already scored a 9.4, it's

Risk,
Originality, and
Virtuosity
that will get us to a 10.

The Reasons Why

I've studied people I know who exhibit true contentment in their lives and it's easy to see that risk-taking is a big part of what they do, that being original is not only important to them but over time seems to come naturally to them, and that doing what they do with flourish and elan—with virtuosity—permeates their performances. I've also observed that many of them don't realize they're using the old gymnastics formula for the perfect 10—but they're using it just the same. And their lives are all the richer for it.

These are people who practice R.O.V. as a matter of course for the simply reason that it enhances their quality of life. They don't do it because they have to, like a gymnast in a competition, or because they heard Peter Vidmar give a speech about it. These are people who choose their own paths and travel them with pride, instinctively using risk, originality and virtuosity.

People like my coach.

Years ago, I was with Mako, helping out at a summer college gymnastics camp he was running. He's over fifty now, and still in better shape than just about anyone I know. He was proud of himself for breaking his personal record for handstand pushups. Most people couldn't do one. Mako Sakamoto had just done 101 (on his way to eventually doing 160!)

He went home that night and told his kids that he'd set the new world record for handstand pushups.

His kids were teenagers. They rolled their eyes.

"Dad," they said, "nobody else *does* handstand pushups."

"I know," said Mako, smiling. "So what's your point?"

INDEX

value, and virtuosity, 99–101
Vidmar, Dick, 16
Vidmar, Dodie, 16
Vidmar, Donna, 116, 124
Vidmar, Doris, 6, 17
Vidmar, John, Jr., 16, 47
Vidmar, John, Sr., 6, 14–18, 150
Vidmar, Melissa, 16
Vidmar, Peter
  on balance in life, 149–153
  competing with illness/injury,
    94–99
  early competitions, 131–132
  family background, 14–18
  gymnastics, choice as sport,
    38–39
  Makoto (Mr. Mako) as coach,
    5–14, 83–84, 93, 96, 98,
    108, 110–111, 116, 154
  mountain biking, 44–47
  new dismount routine, 80–82
  Olympic Games (1984) gold
    medal winner, 1–5,
    105–109
  Olympic Games (1984)
    individual finals, 109–117
  Olympics, lifelong interest in,
    39–40
  post–Olympics career,
    119–127

surfing, 47–51
training approach of, 91–94,
    101–105
World Horizontal Bar
    Champion competition,
    31–37
Vidmar, Tom, 16
virtuosity
  athletic virtuosity examples,
    89–90, 102–116
  and commitment, 92–94
  elements of, 91–92
  and hard work, 87–88
  and value, 99–101

W
Wagner, Berny, 76
Webber, Dewey, 47–48
World Horizontal Bar
    Champion competition,
    31–37
Wright, Wilbur and Orville,
    137–138

X
xerography, 74–75
Xerox Corporation, 75

Z
Ziert, Paul, 49